Improv for Writers

IMPROV
FOR
WRITERS

**10 Secrets to Help Novelists
and Screenwriters Bypass Writer's
Block and Generate Infinite Ideas**

JORJEANA MARIE

TEN SPEED PRESS
California | New York

Copyright © 2019 by Jorjeana Marie

All rights reserved.
Published in the United States by Ten Speed Press, an imprint of Random House,
a division of Penguin Random House LLC, New York.
www.tenspeed.com

Ten Speed Press and the Ten Speed Press colophon are registered trademarks of
Penguin Random House LLC.

Library of Congress Cataloging-in-Publication Data is on file with the publisher.

Trade Paperback ISBN: 978-0-399-58203-5
eBook ISBN: 978-0-399-58204-2

Printed in the United States of America

Cover design by Christine Innes and Sarah Rose Weitzman
Interior design by Sarah Rose Weitzman

10 9 8 7 6 5 4 3 2 1

First Edition

33614081468331

For all kids, big and little;
for Mumsy

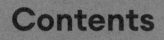

Contents

Preface viii

Introduction 1

PART ONE The Rules

1 *Rule #1*: Say "Yes!" 18

1½ *Rule #1½*: ". . . and" 24

2 *Rule #2*: Be in the Moment 30

3 *Rule #3*: Have No Expectations.................. 37

4 *Rule #4*: Trust 43

5 *Rule #5*: Listen... 48

6 *Rule #6*: Commit 52

7 *Rule #7*: Be an Expert................................... 61

8 *Rule #8*: Be Specific 66

9 *Rule #9*: Set an Intention 72

10 *Rule #10*: Judge Not 76

11 *Bonus Rule*: Conjure Enthusiasm 82

PART TWO Applying Improvisation to Story Elements

12 **Ideas** 96

13 **Settings** 109

14 **Characters** 112

15 **Premises** 143

16 **Dialogue** 148

17 **Plot and Structure** 159

18 **Genres** 169

19 **Theme** 174

20 **Editing** 178

Afterword: Living with These Games 180

Acknowledgments 182

Appendix: Lists 185

Notes 206

About the Author 208

Index 209

Preface

Working in improvisation was not part of the plan. The plan was to be a horror novelist living in a cabin in the woods, channeling Stephen King. But early in high school I discovered theater, and, still in my formative years in NYC, I fell into script writing because of the 24 Hour Plays, wherein a complete production was written, cast, directed/rehearsed, and performed within twenty-four hours.

Hello you!

Doing this, I discovered what it was like to write something on a page and then sit in the back-row darkness of a theater with hundreds of people in the audience, laughing, shifting uncomfortably, and applauding—whew! What a way to begin.

The 24 Hour Plays has really grown in recent years. Now all sorts of celebrities are involved. But it used to be a smaller operation. I was living in the East Village in New York City when I saw a sign from the street and wandered into a building. The place? PS 122. In New York, *PS* stands for *public school*, but this PS had been closed and then reopened, hijacked by creatives and wish makers. The PS was now *Performance Space 122*.

Eddie Izzard appeared there the same week that I first found PS 122, but I didn't know who he was yet. (Yet.) I wandered in past the posters for his performance and found out about the 24-Hour Plays. Right away,

I decided I would participate, and I volunteered to write a play. I think they may have asked me if I was a writer, and since I had been writing sneaky things in my journal long enough to know the answer, I said yes.

The experience was basically the same thing as the games in this book. I was improvising, under a time limit, sitting there in the office at the theater in the middle of the night, becoming the characters at my desk. And almost twenty-four hours later, there I sat squinched between strangers and fellow creators and saw worlds unfold. It was like nothing else. It was so simple, so possible, and—because I had been awake for over twenty-four hours—really, it was like a dream. I had committed to being a writer and letting the creativity flow through me without the critic; I allowed myself to truly have no expectations. This is something I was doing because I wandered into a building and maybe they were short a writer . . . ?

This not having expectations is what allows me to not torture myself: I try my very best to set things up so that I have no expectations. This has been the secret to my personal success. Before I learned to do that, I was frequently blindsided by criticism and redirection and surprises. The 24 Hour Plays was the beginning of me thwarting that inner critic.

It started so simply. Perhaps because I had no expectations, I didn't know enough yet to be afraid or worried what people would think. I just did it. I . . . wait for it . . . wait . . . for it . . . I improvised! I said yes! Doing improv trains you to always say yes. I was mistaken for someone who knew how to write a play and given a chance I've never regretted taking or being given.

This is not just philosophy; there is a real power behind letting go of control as a creative person and trusting your imagination and ability to create. This only really works if you have made the active decision to let go of judgments and commit to the games, the exercises, the character, and to creativity itself. There is much to discover when we do this—mostly, how freeing writing and sharing can be. Just as it is onstage, we can let go on the page.

I'm asking you to trust yourself even in the use of this book. Also, in a sense, to trust me too. I do understand that you may not have ever done improv before, and I really appreciate your interest, courage, bravery, whatever it was that brought us together. I'm grateful for that.

Please know that I have taught so many young and older people improv for many years, and quite a few of them didn't even expect to be doing improv. Some showed up to support their friends in an open class and, at the invite, jumped in. (Talk about trust!)

I'm also a writer. I began as a produced playwright and published poet (in a small kitschy mag that isn't around anymore) in New York City and then of course, I wrote all my own comedy material, so I wrote daily. Which led to writing for animated television shows like *Mickey and the Roadster Racers*, which is driven by funny and fun. Every job, every writer, every character I come across teaches me something.

And in turn, I share that in workshops at high schools, colleges, and libraries around the country and at the studios here in Hollywood. I've taught this very material at workshops at studios, with Scriptwriters Network and other organizations, and we all keep getting the same positive results with these exercises and games. They work.

You are in good hands.

Let's you and I get ready to play our first game. Let's agree that we are going to trust ourselves to create, write, and output mucho. Deal?

Deal from this side.

Pinky shake over here!

Wow! That went so well, let's play another. Maybe a few!

#therearenocoincidences

Introduction

You are an idea machine! Did you know that? Didja? Well, I'm here to confirm, announce, appreciate you—whether you know it or not! This book is for you; an adventure purely of your own making. I'm pleased that you are so interested in being an even more creative, playful person, and I hope to accommodate you on this journey. I consider my job here, on these pages, simply to provide you with a framework. I want to help you build out or build up or simply grease the gears of the idea machine that is you.

I'm going to be honest. I'm pretty silly. I like random absurd things. You might say my own personal idea machine is pretty silly looking, a little cartoony in design—but so am I. (And lucky me, I get to write for kids. So, it works.) But I wouldn't have found my way to where I belong if I didn't understand the rules of improvisation. I learned that I like to create some fun, silly, light things. But on other days, I also like to go darker, and on those projects, my idea machine morphs a little, gets a little more streamlined and angular. So, from one creative person to another, let's agree here and now to feed our machines always, so we are never at a loss, no matter what project, what direction, what story we develop.

I love creating, but I also love teaching. I learn so much from others. A great student makes the best teacher. I have experienced that. To be a good teacher, you must be truly willing to share. To share your toys and information and, yes, secrets. So I'm going to share some secrets that a sect of people (improvisors, comedians, actors of the comedic sort) have been using for thousands of years to come up with stories. And this is serious business, somewhere underneath it all, because a lot of this work is quite successful. Look no further than Shakespeare. He was a poet, playwright, and actor acting in his own plays, coming up with things on the spot (I'm guessing, because my time travel machine isn't complete yet, but probably).

But the road is paved with risk-taking, vulnerability, and going out on a limb. Improvisation is a baring of the soul. The good news is that I'm going to share it with you in a way that doesn't require your going onstage and doing cartwheels, pantomiming making waffles, or pretending you're a pickle manufacturer. Not that doing those things isn't fun for some; quite the contrary. But you will be able to do these exercises from the comfort of your desk. And you will have pages and pages by the time you're done with this book—IF, IF, *IF* you take a chance on me and you, and play the games with commitment, enthusiasm, and a lighthearted attitude.

I'm going to share these secrets with you in as serious a way as I can muster, but I'm also going to provide some silly examples, mostly to encourage you to let go, loosen up, lighten up, fly high, and just—play. And because I can't help myself. I dream in action-adventure and dress like a five-year-old. Sometimes my socks match. Sometimes.

I say all this not to paint the picture of an eccentric writer hacking away at a keyboard (although that is happening) but because I am being vulnerable with you. Most of the samples I give you—heck, all of them—will be written the way I hope you write yours, with trust that they're just that: a sample, a chance to play, a moment of finding out where imagination takes us. And, of course, to illustrate the point of what's being presented.

Because, despite what I like to pretend as I work on sharing all this "gold," this is ALL very, very practical information. It may look like play, but oh boy, give it a chance and you will soon discover some new things about your characters, about your world-building, and (how could you not?) about yourself.

But What Is Improv, Anyway?

Improvisation, or improv for short, is simply writing on your feet. If you improvise instrumental music, you are writing with the language of music. If you improvise with words on a stage, you are writing on your feet, speaking out loud as soon as the words come to you. If you're working with the exercises in this book, you're writing in your chair.

Improvisation was around long before writing. We were acting out stories and making things up. Over time, many styles of storytelling emerged. What we are working with here is based on a more modern take. In the first half of the twentieth century, a woman named Viola Spolin came up with Theatre Games—the basis of many of the improvisation games that we play today. And then, through the decades, her games evolved through the work of many, including her son Paul Sills, the British teacher Keith Johnstone, a fella named Del Close, and Gary Austin, all of them specializing in it and developing it even further. Voilà: improvisation, called improv for short, has become a pop culture phenomenon.

Though modern improv games are at the newer end of theater history, improvisation itself is in many ways the basis of theater as we know it. As I mentioned earlier, Shakespeare's scripts were written *after* the performances.

Many iconic lines in film weren't scripted, either. They were created out of thin air by an actor in the moment, responding to the situation or character in front of them. Jack Nicholson improvised the "Here's Johnny!" line in *The Shining*. "You talkin' to me?!" was Robert De Niro improvising in *Taxi Driver*. Actually, the entire monologue was improvised—the line in the original script was "Travis talks to himself in the mirror." Melissa McCarthy in *Bridesmaids* has some of the funniest moments of the film, and she's making them up!

People think that improv is just *go, don't think, let it all out.* While that may be true, after we've learned some rules, it gets even better. Turns out the rules are very important. Especially if you want to do that thing that people talk about, about knowing them so well that you can then break them? That's good stuff. That's great stuff! So, what follows are some of the rules. Some pertinent improv rules for your writings. Please note that some believe there is only one rule in improv; other schools believe in upward of thirty rules. It's improv, it's art, man—they are all right! But I've studied and taught at a lot of programs and places and don't adhere to just one style or one set of rules. What I am going to do here is share a few li'l secrets that you would have to sit in a roomful of monkeys dancing the waltz (I've seen it) to find out about. I'm going to shyly pass to you on a piece of folded paper (this book) the ones I think are quite useful for writing. I'm a writer myself, and I use the rules of improv to generate new ideas all the time. With this book, I present them to you.

The Three Cs: Character, Commitment, and Creativity

Before I share the rules, here are a few lessons that I have learned through performing and teaching improv. I call them the three Cs: *Character*, *Commitment*, and *Creativity*. These three make up a magical trifecta that acts as a solvent for issues, a foundation, and a net, all at the same time. They are the secret to artistic freedom for creators and portrayers of worlds. For novelists, screenwriters, for any kind of storyteller.

Character

Why is this important? Well, because everything in stories starts with character. Developing that one specific person in your stories is what can connect your work to others. Because writers themselves are characters. You have individual desires, just as much as a character in film or onstage. This is the point I truly want to drive home. There should be no real difference between a character we meet in real life and one we create on the page. They are both meant to be true. Real. Three-dimensional, with all the traits, values, and aspects of any human. Did you ever notice how someone can be so much more to you once you start talking to them, as opposed to just looking at them from a distance? This is exactly why some of the best writers interview and talk to real people. Because that is our job: to depict real people. Not characters; people. We humans, writers, dreamers—we need others. Every novel or script we work on has someone in it. And humans are complex. I want to do my best to be true to the replicating of them in our worlds so that our ideas, conflicts, and stories can really connect, out of truthfulness, no matter the genre or medium—comedy or drama, novel or screenplay.

Before I started attending specific writing programs and seminars (New York University's Dramatic Writing Program at Tisch School of the Arts, Robert McKee's STORY Seminars), all my training was in acting, in theater, film, and improvisation. As acting students, we don't do too much other than observe, interact with, interview, discuss, and analyze people. Some of us even write in our journals as the character or about the character, for pages and pages. This leads me to a theory. Some actors make some of the best screenwriters in town. So many moving and powerful films are created by actors who wrote scripts for themselves. We have some very dynamic characters and roles because the creator was an actor, trained in asking the questions necessary, looking at the world and writing from a different person's viewpoint. Consider Matt Damon and Ben Affleck's *Good Will Hunting* or Nia Vardalos's *My Big Fat Greek Wedding*. An actor's job is to understand characters, so much so that we will live and breathe a character for months for films, or even years for theater and television. I'm not suggesting you turn yourself into an actor. Okay, wait, I kinda am. At least in your office. You already actually do it. Any time you write, you are taking on a certain perspective, and that perspective can be personified as a character. I am just asking you to do this while thinking less. Because when an actor decides to let go of their research and commit their own life to this other human, they replace their own thoughts with the character's thoughts—and perhaps more impactfully, their emotions.

While you may think as the character a fair amount when you are really deep into your story, let's work on letting more emotion come through. This starts with releasing control. I know, I know: releasing control sounds almost absurd, because you do have to pilot the plane and land this story. But can you do it as someone else in parts, releasing love, hate, laughter, and everything in between? I have seen that, as scary as improv can be even to veteran dramatic actors, people from all levels can use it not only to explore character onstage but also to thrive and do work that took them to places they had never dared or dreamed of going. If anyone, at any level, came up to me and said, "I want to understand character better," I would say, without fail, "Get thee to an improvisation class." It is there, without a net, that you will be writing on your feet. And you do so as someone else—hopefully, a character.

I have come to understand there are two types of actors: actors who are like chameleons, changing their facial muscles and wearing prosthetics and morphing into unforgettable people that you can't take your eyes off— such as Philip Seymour Hoffman, Cate Blanchett, or Charlize Theron—and actors who play themselves, or someone like them, in every film. Neither is better; I just really gravitate toward the shapeshifters. Even in fantasy, the actual shapeshifters are fascinating. And this is what I am asking you to do in working through this book: shapeshift from person to person, become someone other than yourself, either sitting at your desk or standing in your office or even when you walk outside to get the mail. Wave to someone as your lead character. Be that person for a moment. If you do some of these improv exercises with commitment, you will learn more about your characters than you ever imagined. Why? Because *you* can only imagine the infinite amount that *you* can imagine. When you start practicing being another person over and over, you have their infinite imagination as well. Infinite imagination times two. Then multiply that by the number of characters in your project that you spend a little extra time to explore in an in-depth way.

But what it comes down to is, character doesn't act alone. To really embody a character like this, we must have a stronger relationship with commitment than we have with criticism.

Commitment

Artists are sensitive. No matter how much swagger we may walk in with, if you tell us you don't like this or that, or suggest something else, we might wonder why what we did wasn't good enough, what's wrong with this piece, or how we can make it better. I'm all for improving, but what I can't stand is doubting my creation. Worse is watching a friend doubt their work. A certain amount of our work simply needs to be good enough that we send that little ship sailing out into the world and give people a chance to respond to it. We'll go into greater detail on commitment in chapter 6, and I will approach this from two angles: first, committing to the decision to be whatever it is you want to be as an artist, and second, committing to letting out and writing whatever wants to come through you, through your characters. Let's commit to the act of writing the way a trained, confident actor walks onto the stage, committed to their character. Be your character as you let them talk, unfold, exist.

This awakens the imagination still living inside all of us, the imagination we embodied as children. We commit to our work the same way a kid decides to be a gnome or a horse or a dragon. Kids at play don't doubt. They don't ask, "Would a knight really do this?" No, they just run at full blast and, well, become dragons. They commit to their play. We can do the exact same thing.

When I started writing professionally, I noticed that I lacked some of the common challenges my writer friends have—specifically, in dealing with the inner critic and the paralysis that accompanies it. I believe I skipped this one because of my experience performing and teaching improv. My job, my paid profession for years has been to make things up. On. The. Spot. Writing came naturally after that.

So, though I do face challenges like any other writer, I've never experienced any form of writer's block (knock on wood and knock it hard). Commitment has a lot to do with confidence, and confidence has everything to do with writer's block. In improv, there's not a lot of room for blocks. Improvisation is the antidote to criticism. Confidence is required every step of the way. You create, create, and create so much that soon you discover you are a creating machine, that it is your one purpose and there is no point to judging it, only doing it, on repeat until you fall asleep at the end of the day worn out from so much activity. So worn out you could care less what your inner critic or the *New York Times* or the *Florida Sun* thinks, because you did what you meant to do. You made something with your mind. You, master of worlds! You, slayer of beasts! You, improvisor!

This also resolves issues with dialogue. Once I'm committed to be the character and letting them talk, I don't judge myself so harshly. I simply am the character. I let them take over, and what they say or do or want is a great place to follow. I commit to the character, follow their lead, and trust fall into bliss. (By the way, trust fall—where you fall backward into the arms of others with your eyes closed, trusting they will catch you—is an improv exercise we will not be doing, because as writers we're often alone and this exercise could end badly. We'll not have any of that.)

With commitment, you kill criticism—annihilate it, shrivel it up like a prune. Because commitment is a metaphorical safety net. When you commit, you know you gave it everything you had, and the rest is like hash browns—something on the side you don't really need.

Character and commitment in improvisation open us all up to a whole new world of spontaneous creativity.

Creativity

Have you felt the universal creative stream that's out there? How it exists and runs through you from time to time if you're lucky or, often, if you're really plugged in?

Look around at your friends and family and pick out the "creative" ones. Maybe it's even you. Probably it is. If you've picked up this book,

I'm gonna guess it's you. Now, the so-called "creative" people didn't get more than anyone else. I am going to offer some suggestions to develop, expand, and express creativity, to tap into that stream. Take what you like and toss what you don't. Use what works. Forget the rest.

Things like self-doubt and self-consciousness are the enemy of creativity. If you want to be more creative, it's totally possible. It just goes hand in hand with getting out of your head, away from criticism and into the natural play state you had as a child. We start to forget how creative we really are—maybe because of comments, maybe because we're busy doing other things, maybe for a lot of reasons—but let this subject of making things up and playing games be a reminder that it's all very important work. There is a real, tangible thing at the end of each of these games—pages; pages and pages and pages of creativity. I have them, I've seen them, I've done them. They exist. They come from brave people in workshops and friends and folks from my writer's group. And every time someone is willing to share their pages from these games, I am floored, every single time, at how very, very creative they are. You can learn structure from great teachers. You can't "learn" creativity. You just *are* creative. Maybe you forgot that for a moment. Welcome back. Welcome home. This is who you are, who you were as a child. You are creative in your way. Just as when you write you use your own voice, being creative doesn't mean using all the crayon colors from the 64-pack; it means using the colors you pick to make the thing you are inspired to make.

And there are so many ways to get creative and get inspired. We're going to track some of them here, but there are other people out there who will help you tap into creativity too. You just have to look for them. You'll know who they are, because you'll get your own ideas when you're around them or reading their work. It will be different for everyone.

Also, you don't have to look outside for creativity. That's just one way. The other is settling into the idea that *you* are where fantastic, unique ideas come from and that you can turn them on at will like a faucet. You can go fishing in a giant pool of reflections for them. You can hitch a ride along the idea superhighway. You can dip your pail in the ancient well of wisdom. You are the start of something.

My point is: Let's play some games, my new friend! Let's let our natural creative side shine in everything we do.

As you move through this book, through your writing career, know that you can turn up your own creativity and imagination as many notches as you want just by approaching life with a curiosity—the "what if" factor so many successful authors talk about. That's improvisation. You're already doing it if you play that game. You're already creative—now it's just time to IMPROVISE!

How to Use This Book

Most of the games and exercises included here do exist out there in the beautiful world of improvisation. Some of these are games I've invented over the years; some are a version of a classic game. Regardless, I am not going to ask you to do any performing. Although that can be a whole lot of fun, this is not about that. Also, you already know how to do this. You perform every time you walk out the front door. You change character as easily as any great actor when you go from an uncomfortable work party to a rollicking concert to Thanksgiving at someone else's house. And you, my new friend, do even more than the regular citizen out there. You're making up entire universes. You're a writer! It's what you do. You just aren't doing it live in front of a whole bunch of people; nevertheless, you *are* doing it. You're performing all the characters with their traits and flaws and emotions inside your head. Whoa!

All I am giving you are some extry bits, tools, and games that you can access whenever you like. They're out there—and so much more, too— for you to use as much or as little of as you want.

I invite you to play these games over and over, to even adjust them to suit yourself. The people who improvise consistently begin to make up their own games, their own forms (as they are called in the improv biz) that allow them to explore or express the world and their viewpoint

QUICK TIP: Trust Your Impulses

When you sit down to do these games, ideas and thoughts will pop into your brain. Go with them. Later on you can play with ignoring that first step and digging deeper, but until then, use that first seed that springs up, and water it.

in a new way. Once you have a real grasp of the rules, the way the games work, and how they actually begin to change you, grow you, rewire you, you too can bend them to your needs.

It's kind of amazing how flexible the art form is. And it is an art form. Well, it's also a philosophy, and it's a kind of way to live life as well. (See what I mean about its being all flexy?)

This is a workbook for the work of writing. Getting into a great space for creating, wringing out our imagination, deepening our understanding of people and therefore of characters, and having a stockpile of tools to move the work forward. Letting go of how things should be, how you should act, where you want projects or characters ending up, what you need the process, the project, the result, even the beginning of the story to be. Improvisation has to do with letting go of all the ideas of how all things should be. And then what? Improvisation is all about trusting. Trusting that things will be okay, the story will find its way, the characters will be as they should be, minds will be blown, your head will produce all the right words at the right moment, and your hands and fingers, typing or handwriting, will do the work that must be done. Improvisation is trusting that the story you are going to tell is the one that needs to be told. I am asking you to let go, explore, discover, create. And then to not judge it. If we've done nothing else in life, we're ahead of the curve. And that's a great place to be. Even when others complain, like in school, that you're ruining the curve. Who cares? Let go. Explore. Discover. Create.

Some of these games may seem esoteric, so I provide some examples, and of course, you can always look up most of these games online—improv

On this new journey, there is something very important to keep in mind: Writing can be joyous, fulfilling, and—dare I say it?—FUN! We can torture ourselves for art—and plenty of people do—but acting styles have moved away from wounded souls digging into their psyche and toward the modern actor, who works with improv, being present. Actors often have a good time. We love acting, because it is like the make-believe we did when we were children, and we are harnessing that, even when it's a serious role. Approach the games and exercises in this book with the same attitude: you're playing, and it's fun!

schools throughout the world play them or sometimes a version of them under another name. You can find more info about each on my website: jorjeanamarie.com.

Please note there will be some silly games. I'll include why I would ask you to do these seemingly silly things and the infinite gains you can get from doing so. I also include some more serious games, but please, approach everything with your fun hat on. If you're not in a good mood, do whatever it takes to lift your spirits, then play.

Be forewarned: these games do have a side effect of raising spirits. Because . . . games!

Feel free to read this book in order or skip around trying things. I recommended reading it through from the beginning, but when you come across something that you want to try, get out your pen and paper or 'puter and give the exercises and games a go. Do what moves you. For instance, if you are in desperate need of some help with a current project regarding your character, please skip to that chapter. And skip to the loo while you're at it.

If you're working on a novel or script and you want to do some exploratory work on your villain, check out that section later. Take your villain and put him or her in some situations listed there, or make up your own.

Please, run with it! This is a book on improvising, after all. I like to mix things up and change and try different things—always. Let's play like we are five and commit to our pretending. There are so many ways to play improv and use the different games. What matters most, in the end, is that we are all playing, that we are all free. That we are creating.

Even though you'll use a timer in almost all the exercises, an occasional pause is okay, especially when you feel something is barreling toward you, an idea is forming . . . you can't just write over it. Yes, the point is to become adept at coming up with an idea on the spot, but, just like onstage, you're not meant to be talking a mile a minute all the way through a scene; nor are any of your characters, unless that's a choice you've made. No, you take a breath, you listen to the other person, you stare longingly at the sandwich you've ordered and can see is finally coming your way. Sometimes we wait. Sometimes there is silence. But there's a big difference between having a moment of revelation hit you and not knowing what to say or write.

You can try it this way: when first working through the exercise, go for speed, get words on the page; then later, challenge yourself to take longer with the exercises, adjust the timer in whichever direction is harder for you. Let the layers that improv can give you arrive and become a part of your process, especially as we move into the second half of the book and the games become more involved.

The games are meant to be played over and over and over. I still do the same games as when I first started, but now I find new ways to grow within them, to challenge myself, even if it feels uncomfortable. And eventually they feel like a tool, and you will be able to take them and change them. Just as I have for you here, just as has been happening with improv for thousands of years.

As you go through these pages, you'll find you're drawn to certain games and exercises, just like you're drawn to different styles of art. At some points, I'll ask you to step outside of your comfort zone. I have found in art and life that it's very good to step beyond where I am comfortable.

Most improv consists of warm-ups, exercises, and games. We do warm-ups before we get to work playing the games, so those are important prep work to do, but guess what? They can be fun too! Exercises are used to strengthen a particular improv muscle, like agreement or not being critical. And games are played to come up with stories, characters, and ideas. You know what games are 'cause you've got your game on!

After each game or warm-up, I'll say "Good job" or "Good stuff" because in my writer's co-op of over forty writers, there is one woman who, no matter what anyone writes, always says "Good job" at the end of her thoughtful critique. I think she's saying "Good job" because it's scary to bring pages in, so she's acknowledging the courageous act. And I loved her for it immediately. It caught my ear, and since I've also taught at many schools, libraries, and workshops where I give no criticisms (what's the point with improv, anyway?), I thought I'd include it here. So, get ready to work—uh, play—and I'll holler at you "Good job" or "Nice work" for playing the game. Because you could just read the book. But what fun would that be?

Now, I sometimes put off playing the games; I sometimes resist. I think that's just part of the work. We have to show up. But every time I play a game, I want to play another, and I am once again under the spell of the magic that is improvisation.

There will be little **QUICK TIPS** along the way, but if they don't answer your questions, feel free to come on over to www.jorjeanamarie .com and shoot me a message or look through articles on improv rules and games there. Oh! There a couple of sections of writing with a partner. Sometimes we have writing partners, so I've included some games just for when that happens on projects or when you can snag someone from your writers' group to join you for an exercise.

In the acting world, improvising is often called "writing on your feet." So I feel confident the improv community supports my sharing the rules and games of improvisation with you. Improvisors are such warm, charming, smart, fun people who instinctively rally around each other and lift each other up. Share and share alike—it's what we do! *Mi casa es su casa*

THINGS YOU WILL NEED

- **A timer.** Please note that you may want to adjust the amount of time, perhaps because you're a very fast or slow writer or typist or calligrapher—my time limits aren't set in stone. None of this is. Goodness, what a heavy book this would be!

- **Your imagination.**

- **Something to write on or in.** Use a specific journal or file.

- **Willingness.** Let go of your own judgment about what you or anyone else creates.

- **Lists.** There are lists for you to use at the back of the book. Feel free to add to them by filling in the blanks at the ends.

- **Something to write with.** Use pen, paper, notebook, computer, tablet.

- **Recording device (optional).** You may be the kind of person who is more comfortable talking aloud, acting out on your own, speaking—so go ahead and record yourself playing these games, becoming characters, describing scenery, and so on.

and all that. So you have total permission to be here, even though we are getting into some secrets! We will apply these rules and play games, and you will come up with a slew of ideas. You will get so good at this, you too can create confidently at a moment's notice.

Here's the beauty of all this fooling around and acting like a goofball (I mostly use myself as an example when I say that term; many writers are quite refined and elegant). The beauty is, you can change it all later. You, my new friend, writer of things, creator of compelling stuff—you can go back and edit. What I'm saying is, "PLAY WITH ME!!" You have absolutely nothing to lose, and freedom, joy, and exhilaration at new discoveries to gain. Everything to gain: The world is yours. Cuz, um, you make it up and say so.

#letsplay

PART ONE

The Rules

Rule #1: Say Yes!

We're starting right here with the big jumbotron mega important rule and a quote by a powerful improv teacher, Keith Johnstone. This rule is the head honcho of moving the scene forward—always. Some schools even believe this is the only rule you will ever need: *Say yes.*

Agree to play the game, agree to your scene partner, agree to the reality of whatever is being presented—just, for the love of all that is good, agree. Find a way to let go of the human need that we have been practicing since we were children learning to talk and found we could scream "NO!" at the top of our lungs. Today is all about yes. Improvisation is all about yes. And what does that mean? Find a way to be in alignment with everything around you, to agree. Improvisation is not about conflict or disagreeing. It flies in the face of plot structure but, in some crazy way, makes everything better.

In traditional improv, agreement is the key to building a scene with whomever you find yourself onstage with. And inevitably, it is the first thing beginning improvisors buck up against. Denying is a very common response and one I have certainly found myself doing. Someone would make me a teapot. Instead of thanking my improv partner for this gift and

QUICK TIP: Be Playful!

Play is one of those things some of us do less and less as time goes by. I don't think that's because there's less to be silly about. There's always plenty of reason to play, but after we stop getting "play" breaks in school (recess) and teachers stop encouraging us and parents get annoyed by it and bosses don't have time for it . . . well, before you know it, play is just—well, it's just gone. It may take repeated attempts, and I'll do my best to remind you throughout, but improv, at its core, is made up of games. And you know what to do in a game. Yes, play!

running with it ("Well, I'm glad you joined me for high tea! Sit down, and I'll pour you a spot") so that we can be off to the races with our scene and agreement, other green performers and I will look the person giving said information in the eye and say: "NO! You're crazy! I'm not a teapot, you moron."

We don't always make our disagreement so obvious, of course. Sometimes it's very subtle. For instance, a woman is washing dishes in the scene, and I walk right through her imaginary sink, destroying her reality and the audience's. In that moment, I am not saying yes; I am screaming no. The whole audience sees it, she knows it, and our creation is dead.

Saying yes can be just as subtle. For instance, I could take a moment to be present, aware of what my scene partner is building, and then, without a word, walk around her marble countertop. Better yet, I could pick up a plate and put it away while we continue with the scene. And trust me, it's not about the sink—the sink is just the background. The scene is about us and how we feel about each other. How we are saying yes to each new bit of information that either one of us is coming up with next.

This improv rule has helped me immensely. And I don't mean just in my acting work or my writing work—I mean in my life. Again, improv is a philosophy. And here's how this philosophy works: when your partner onstage offers you an idea, a character trait about yourself, an imaginary telephone call, it is paramount to say yes. It's paramount that you appreciate the idea, accept the trait, take the call because it moves the scene forward. Someone is offering up gifts of information, and those gifts are sending us somewhere.

Maybe you don't like the gift you receive. That doesn't matter one iota, because now it's out there in front of the audience, and they have heard it. There is only one thing to do now: agree. And agree we must, or the scene stops.

By saying no, what exactly are we doing? We're destroying an artistic creation, introducing doubt, insecurity, judgment, fear, or whatever it is that is keeping us from saying yes.

How do we start moving our scenes forward? We start finding common ground. I don't think of it as giving in and being a "yes man." It's bigger than that. It's saying, "I hear you, I'm receiving your signal—and guess what? I'm supporting you." That's all your partner wants. That's all you want! Anything else tends to make the audience uncomfortable. A loud "No, there's no call for me, that's your hand, not a phone" might get a laugh from the audience, but it's not the kind of laugh anyone wants to get. This laugh is laced with discomfort and traces of knowledge that what we're watching just isn't right. We can do better. So as much as we can, in that split second when so much is happening, we accept

Yes!

the information. We receive it. We take it in like a stray cat at our door, and we prepare for the next step. In this situation, that is our job.

Drawing parallels between improvisation onstage and improvisation in writing is not difficult. As writers, we have a chance to say yes in every moment. The thought that arrived, the idea, the bit of whatever that just appeared—that is an offering to you. When I accept these thoughts, I do my best to not judge them but to just jot them down. Sometimes I can't help it and I get really excited about something, but enthusiasm is okay. What we're trying to avoid is the vetoing of ideas, the stopping of momentum, the general disregard that ends our work for that moment, that hour, that day.

Onstage, "No" spreads like a disease, infecting everything. In writing, it's just the same. "No" spoils everything in its path. It makes children cry! And the antidote is simple; it's one word. Say it with me now, please. Say it aloud. Start saying it every chance you get, as soon as ideas come, when you sit down to write, when a chance comes along to practice this most practical exercise.

Say Yes!

Now I am going to ask you to get out of your head, to let go of judgment and try something you may have never done before. There's truly no reason to judge, because these places don't really exist. Have fun!

#letthegamesbegin

QUICK TIP: Peas In the Pod

If you want to create a scene with more *yes*, more fun, and your characters are really getting along, take a tip from improv's peas in a pod–type scenes, in which one character in the scene is doing something and another character joins in and does what they are doing with just as much enthusiasm. Two pilots working a flight plan, two monkeys grooming each other, two killers sharing techniques. Set the timer for five minutes and try it on any characters you want!

GAME: Yes, Let's

Let's play "Yes, Let's," where you and a friend or friends go on the vacation of a lifetime. Yes, it will be to a place that doesn't exist, but it promises to be unlike any trip you've ever taken.

WHY ON EARTH WOULD WE DO THIS?

We're dipping our toe in the water of writing without thinking, following where our imagination and inspiration take us. The point of all these games is to free up your writing, to free up your mind, make it work in a different way, to flex and build muscles you were unaware that you could. As a side effect, you may find you're suddenly much more involved in conversations at dinner parties.

As you'll find with all the other rules, there's no planning beforehand. Maybe you'll find this easy, maybe not. Either way, it's okay. Keep in mind, nothing needs to make sense; if it does make some, even better. We'll work on that. We're just getting warmed up with a simple exercise and beginning to practice letting the writing flow and agreeing with ourselves and our own ideas.

At minimum, this is a book of prompts; at its max, ideally, this is a whole new way of working that is as useful as it is playful, as fun as it is eye-opening, as freeing as it is full of creative fundamentals.

The example that follows is a little silly because I want to encourage that. Please join me in exploring your illogical mind. We have plenty of exercises that will come later that can get you writing. Some serious pieces. Explore it all. But for now, for always, play. Sit down somewhere you feel quite comfortable, ready to write.

- Choose a number from 1 through 30.
- Grab the corresponding item from the Settings (Made-Up) list, page 202.
- Select a person from your life or your celebrity crush to go with you.

- Write/type at the top of your page: Yes, let's go to [fill in a destination]!
- Set a timer for five minutes.
- Begin describing this exciting vacation. (Don't stop to think!)
- Each sentence written must begin with "Yes, let's . . ." and end with an exclamation point. If you were acting this out onstage, you would be yelling by the end, so do your best and get excited! Go on! No spending limits, anywhere, anytime. The sky's the limit—but not really! Go on, plan a trip to an unknown galaxy, a made-up island, a nonexistent wonder of the world.
- Keep the pen, pencil, or typing fingers moving rapidly until the timer goes off. Five sentences are great; so are twenty.

Great work!

EXAMPLE

I selected number 13 and turned to the Made-Up Places list:

Yes, let's go to a moon colony in fifty years! Yes, let's take a few floaties and pool noodles for the gravity pool! Yes, let's bring our blue and red rocket covered flannel pajamas—I heard they keep it cool at night! Yes, let's pack extra peanut butter packets—they do get skimpy with rations! Yes, let's bring dancing shoes for the big Moon Dance Festival! Yes, let's pack an extra fancy dress for dinner with the head of NEW NASA! Yes, let's remember our acne medicine, since the dryness there is known to cause breakouts! Yes, let's bring our journals with keys, since sometimes the staff gets a little snoopy; I read it on the Moon Travels blog comments!

1½

Rule #1½: "... and"

This is not just a half rule. It's kinda everything. It holds hands nicely with the first rule of saying yes, of agreeing. The second half of the essential "Yes," the "... and," is also about *agreement*—not only do you agree to go along with the story placed in front of you, but you also agree to *add* to it. Good conversations in life are like this. Our job as writers is to always be moving forward, adding information, adding words, adding dialogue, molding, creating. All subsequent information added to a scene builds on the agreement established when "Yes" becomes an action and not just a word.

When you meet someone and are drawn to them, you don't just say, "Yes!" You say, "Yes, hello. You are looking ravishing in that gold lamé." Or "Yes, hello. It's so nice to meet a fellow lover of O'Keeffe—I saw you admiring that print from across the room."

Then we have somewhere to go, as opposed to: "Yes ... umm." That gets us nothing. Well, it gets us agreement, so at least we're on the right path, but come on ... let's add some veggies to the stew. Like:

"Yes, I've been looking forward to our settlement meeting *all* day."

"Well, well. Then let's get these proceedings underway. Excellent choice in a blazer, Barbara."

These two lines can be said many ways with infinite meanings, but we have at least some idea of what's going on. Not just "umm." "Umm" is that feeling you get sitting in front of your computer, knowing you should be doing something, but you're saying "umm." And that's a start—at least we've gotten to the desk this day—I'm just suggesting you play the "and" part. Go, go, go!

This is your opportunity to frontload your art, to give over everything you have, to share, to invite spirit to move with you as you contribute! All this "Yes . . . and" rule is asking you to do is to add information—getting it into our heads, getting it onto that page. Information can be breezy and flowy, like a caftan. The only requirements are to add information and to not judge it.

In some improvisation schools and theater companies, this action is called "gifting." Onstage, I might gift my scene partner with some information to tell her what we've been sweating over and digging up with these imaginary shovels for twenty seconds already! On the page, I gift my story with additional information that I come up with on the spot, based on the prompt of a game or word. Much like onstage, that scene was prompted by the audience's suggestion.

Please give your wild-eyed scene partner the same kind of gift. How does this *muy importante* role translate from the stage for writers? Easily. You are giving to your audience, your readers, your fans. You are giving of yourself. And yes, it's different from showing your support and building with a teammate onstage, but you are doing the same on the page—you are adding information. You are letting the story flow, letting it roll and wander and weave.

You are sitting and writing in character and not editing, not doing extensive research, and not focusing on peppering in that information in just the right amount for the reader. You are contributing to the story and making sure it moves ahead. Many writers know how to do those things, but can you do it without stopping to judge yourself? Can you trust that the editing will come later?

Mastering the ability to create forward momentum while writing sounds dern good to me and is the outcome of applying this gem. This is a chapter for practicing what it really means to be adding quality information to a creation. (Is it just me, or did that rhyme?)

This rule and the accompanying game "Ad Agency" helps you to build up this important reflex so that saying yes becomes quite natural. So we learn to just throw information out there without judging it, which is important in at least one phase of writing—the start. Proceeding with an idea without stopping yourself becomes innate after practicing this.

Let it be!

In this game I am going to ask you to take on a character: an advertising genius developing ways to sell a never-before-seen product. This one calls for a little acting at your workstation—and no one will even know what you're up to. Just pretend you're a high-powered ad exec. And if you really are a high-powered ad exec, be one from the fifties, à la *Mad Men*. And if you really are like one of those characters and lived through that time, choose someone from the future or the 1890s. Ya dig? We're exploring being someone else for a few minutes.

#dontleavemehangin

QUICK TIP: Double Check

Check that all sentences start with "Yes, and." If you had many that didn't, try this one again. When we play in the theater with "outsies," each time you start a sentence and don't begin with "yes, and," you're out of the game and someone else takes your place, so be strict on this until it's second nature to you.

GAME: Ad Agency

This is played just like advertising agents do when they are spit-balling ideas. Just be sure to start every sentence you write with: "Yes, and. . . ." End with an exclamation point. It can be easy to forget to start each sentence this way, but we're training our brain to learn to agree more, when the natural thing can be to judge and say, "No, that's a pretty stupid idea, Bob!" So it's an important habit to begin forming.

WHY ON EARTH WOULD WE DO THIS?

This game is developing the agreement muscle, which for some of us has actually atrophied. It's a gateway to going along with the first thing your awesome brain thinks up, rather than mowing it down with "Nah!" Finding ways to work this into your day-to-day writing can change the way you work. It's great to do over and over—especially if you notice that you stop yourself a lot. We want to strengthen your ability to write and write without judgment. Now you can consistently play through and see what else is inside your mind, what other interesting idea sits up in the ether, waiting for you to grab it. Once you find agreement within and support the idea's arrival on the page, more ideas will gently poke their heads up, over, around the corner, no longer fearing a good bopping back, back, back!

- Choose a number from 1 through 30.
- Find the corresponding prompt from the Products (Made-Up) list, page 200.
- Set the timer for five minutes.
- Become a powerful creative (even sit up taller!) who lets the ideas flow on ways to sell this thing!
- Remember, start each sentence with agreeing and adding info! "Yes . . . and!"
- Start writing.
- Write until the timer goes off. (Of course, you can finish out the thought—or keep going if you're inspired to!)

Nice work!

Yes, and we can market this using Jackson Pollock's paintings! Yes, and we'll involve his estate and would work out a deal with them! Yes, and we can even shoot some commercials with them, aiming the Paint Splatterer! Yes, and we can even auction those off at charity events and create ads about that to garner goodwill! . . . (and so on, until the timer goes off).

GAME: Pitch It

I hope "Ad Agency" was a lot of fun. Let's do it again, but with a variation. This time, you're going to come up with the title of a movie that's never been made before. Go on! You can do it! If you don't have anything in a few seconds, feel free to meander through your favorite genre of movies at the library or in your streaming queue. I like romantic comedies, so I'll do one of those in my example. But if you like westerns, come up with the title of a western that's never been made. We're gonna write the pitch for that movie the "Yes . . . and!" way.

Use the provided list and pitch it to imaginary film/television executives. I would love for you to try the game next time with your own made-up versions of list items if you use the lists a lot, *or* ask for one from a stranger. Now there's a special moment!

WHY ON EARTH WOULD WE DO THIS?

We're practicing coming up with more and more ideas and letting them all exist at once. There's no reason to judge, because it's all made up. It doesn't exist. Be sure you don't start thinking or hesitating—this is silly and freeing and all about agreeing with the *first* thing you think of and adding to it!

Our minds can provide infinite information when we remove the filter. Feel free to play twice. Who knows? You might just come up with the next great movie idea and *really* start pitching it!

- Choose a number from 1 through 25.

- Find the corresponding prompt from the Movies That Have Not Been Made . . . Yet! list, page 195.

- Set the timer for five minutes.

- Become a powerful creative writer with many similar movies produced to great acclaim. Let the ideas flow, and pitch this movie! You can even add real or made-up celebrities to star in it.

- Remember, start each sentence with agreeing and adding info, "Yes . . . and!"

- Write until the timer goes off.

Good job!

QUICK TIP: Separate but Together

Try playing these games with a writer friend. I really enjoy playing the games with other people at the same time. Those times have become really memorable to me and meaningful. This kind of cocreating energy is very powerful to me, even if we're working on our own projects, just at the same table. Not only do you have the timer, but you have an extra dose of accountability because your friend is there with you and you have their support. Afterward, be sure to share what you each wrote. You'll amaze each other. No critiques necessary at this stage. Start a movement and get a whole group together some night!

> Oh, now, now, now, the only now, and above
> all now, and there is no other now but thou
> now and now is thy prophet.
> —ERNEST HEMINGWAY

Rule #2:

Be in the Moment

Improvisors are thinking about many things at one time, but the only time that matters is now.

If we are not present, we cannot listen. If we aren't listening, how can we hear the story of the world around us? Of our own inner voice? Of something bigger than ourselves? Of our ancestors? Of history? Of the couple who triggers our romantic comedy? Of the president who fuels our next political thriller? Whatever it is that we want to be writing about, we must be there in order to listen.

Here are some tools that I've found most useful for getting into the great "hear" and now.

- **Breathing exercises**

- **Meditation**

- **Sitting in silence**

There is only now

This chapter presents a simple meditation for prepping to write. You may already have a preferred meditation practice or ritual. If you are new to this idea, you can start out with a very short time period—five minutes? That's what I began with many years ago when I was seeking a way to get centered. Carve out five minutes for yourself. Setting a timer with a soft bell sound is a good way to gauge how long you've been meditating and takes the focus off of watching the time. Relax. Sit comfortably. Close your eyes. Inhale slowly, exhale slowly. Repeat, lengthening the breath. When thoughts come in, let them pass. That's a very normal experience, and even people who have been meditating for a long time will tell you, that is the game, to let thoughts come and go. Come and go, go, go. . . .

If you do want to dive in further, I recommend seeking out an experienced practitioner. I've gone to many different meditation groups over the years, and I've tried a lot of different styles. Just like writing, laughing, and pie-making, there are many different ways to do it, and yours is going to be unique, just as it should be.

Meditation has been around for thousands of years; everyone from the religious to artists to scientists have been known to use it. I love Voltaire's description: "One day in the year 1666, Newton went into the country, and seeing fruit fall from a tree (as his niece, Madame Conduit, has informed me), entered into a profound train of thought as to the causes which could lead to such a drawing together or attraction."

More recently Suze Yalof Schwartz, creator of Unplug Meditation in Los Angeles, tells us: "Meditation is a practice that teaches you to unplug from distraction and experience the present moment. . . . According to the National Science Foundation, the average person has approximately fifty thousand thoughts a day. The thoughts just keep coming, all day long, stealing our attention away from the present moment. The problem is, the present moment is kind of important, because it's where your life is actually happening. Not five minutes ago, not five minutes from right now—right here, right now. That's all there is."

If meditation doesn't interest you, would you consider sitting in silence? Or driving in silence. Julia Cameron wrote in *The Artist's Way*: "Steven Spielberg claims that his very best ideas have come to him as he was driving the freeways. This is no accident. Negotiating the flow of traffic, he was an artist immersed in an oncoming, ever altering flow of images. Images trigger the artist's brain. Images fill the well."

So sit in silence or drive about or walk about, and get ready, because ideas are always on their way, and I think, like trouble, if you're looking for it, you'll find it.

Finally, to be in the present moment, you can always just decide to be there, right? It is, after all, the decision to enter the now. Sometimes the simplest answer is the best.

I have found these exercises very helpful in centering and grounding before beginning my work—and the work has always flowed more easily when I've started my day or writing session this way. And sometimes being in the now happens even faster and easier once the first three have been practiced. Totally up to you. Choose one (or all) and let's take a moment together. Get comfortable. Ready? Ommmmmmmm....

#writingisbreathing

WARM-UP EXERCISE: Every Breath You Take

Isn't it funny that sometimes we don't breathe deeply until someone tells us to? So, go ahead, take a deep breath. Doesn't that feel good?

WHY ON EARTH WOULD WE DO THIS?

These exercises will leave you prepared to journey into your work—your own story—and live there as an observer or, better yet, as a participant. The power of these three tools has been scientifically proven and artistically experienced. These are tools that actors, athletes, comedians, public speakers, and the like use all the time, and they can help us writers align ourselves with the spring from which ideas flow.

A whole new world opens right up when we are present. And we have the tools to create ourselves a tailored program for arriving at our desk motivated, focused, and ready to go. Suddenly we can better observe what is happening around us—and get it onto the page.

- Slowly inhale for a count; slowly exhale for two counts.
- Slowly inhale for two; slowly exhale for four counts.
- Continue to higher numbers as your breath allows.
- Great!
- With practice you can expand the counts quite a bit. You can also practice pausing. . . .
- Inhale slowly for three counts.
- Hold for three.
- Exhale slowly for three counts.
- Repeat four or five times.
- Explore lengthening your counts and pauses to learn better breath control.

Nicely done!

EXERCISE: See It, Be It!

The acting world has so many warm-ups like this. They're really great for focus, relaxation, or imagination. Plenty of writers actually already do this. And so does every child who ever lived. It's really just daydreaming. And it leads to inspiration. If we don't give ourselves room to do this seemingly simple thing as an adult, we have inadvertently shut creativity out. Envisioning is easier for some but is important for all of us to spend at least some time doing. Don't skip this. Especially if it's hard for you.

WHY ON EARTH WOULD WE DO THIS?

It has been proven that visualizing works for athletes, entrepreneurs, and inventors; indeed, it is an important part of their coaching and strategy. Creative people in all fields are masters of visualizing. But they must make time and space for it. When we visualize, we open a door wide for imagination, for possibility. But we don't always make time for it. Or even believe it has any power. Believe, new friend. Believe. You are the creator of worlds, and here is a moment in time to begin doing exactly that.

- Choose a place that you have been to that you have loved with all your heart. Maybe it's the forest in between the great redwoods or a villa in Italy or a childhood park. Feel free to also play this game with more imagination than memory by using your own made-up setting, or select one from Settings (Made-Up) on page 202.

- Close your eyes and put yourself there.

- See the details of this place; see the reasons why you love going there. Feel the way the air feels—maybe you can even smell blossoms? Is there a flower to touch?

- Linger. Spend some moments in this place and really do your best to see everything you can with your mind's eye. Even if it's a made-up, magical place, allow yourself to fully experience an immersion into this place and, if you can, go beyond just seeing and allow yourself to feel, to sense every detail you can with your six senses.

look at you go!

EXERCISE: Meditation

Now let's try another exercise. When I do this one, it changes my entire day; I'm somehow both more relaxed and more aware—meditation, again. I first discovered meditation as a teen doing yoga, and though I've been intermittent with my own meditation practice, these past few years I've been more consistent, and I've also been having the time of my life. Coincidence? Not likely. I'm throwing out a very simple exercise, but please keep in mind there are so many great teachers and courses in this subject that if you are getting something out of it, I highly recommend you study with someone with experience. It takes your practice to another level entirely.

WHY ON EARTH WOULD WE DO THIS?

Filmmaker David Lynch says, "I'm a meditator, and the idea of that is to expand consciousness by clearing the machines of consciousness, which is the nervous system, and the greater the consciousness—I think, in the analogy of fishing—the deeper your hook can go to catch the bigger ideas." By doing this meditation before you write, you're opening yourself up to those big ideas!

- **Find a comfortable place in your work space or home where you won't be disturbed and sit comfortably.**
- **Set your timer for five minutes.**
- **Close your eyes.**
- **Inhale and exhale with a focus on your breath. If your mind wanders, that's okay; you can always pull your attention back to the breath.**

- Meditate until the timer goes off.
- Perhaps next time you can do seven minutes!

Good job!

QUICK TIP: Sip!

If meditation is too formal for you, a dear friend told me when I was struggling, it can be as easy as taking your tea or coffee outside and sitting quietly on your favorite bench for a few minutes. These moments alone help us get centered, and I have found I always have more ideas, more to give, more, more when I start my day this way or do this just before writing.

> I wanted a perfect ending. Now I've learned,
> the hard way, that some poems don't rhyme,
> and some stories don't have a clear beginning,
> middle, and end. Life is about not knowing,
> having to change, taking the moment, and
> making the best of it, without knowing what's
> going to happen next.
>
> —GILDA RADNER

Rule #3:

Have No Expectations

The No Expectations rule is about not controlling the things around you, not expecting something to turn out in a certain way, and being happy with what you have. Being so happy that you then find the flow. The flow of the scene, the story, the character's trajectory, of life. It's about staying open. Things may or may not go a certain way, and that's okay.

This mindset is just as important to creativity as it is to life in general. If we can be open to where the characters, the stories, the finger paints take us, we can create more than we ever thought possible. A grand adventure awaits if we can stop stopping the go train. This is also another way to say yes—to the idea that sounds kinda crazy, to the whim that might take you to your epic tale, to the unknown. It can be scary, but that is part of our job, isn't it? To peel back the layer and see the terrible thing underneath? We'll never know what's there if we don't look, if we don't deviate from our schedule/path/rigid ideas and outlines. We can always turn around if we don't like where it's taking us, but we can't just look away. So peer down the dark alley; discover what your main character is really thinking by spending time as them; don't look for answers so much as recognize them when they appear. We can't recognize new possibilities when we are spending all our energy controlling one idea.

We can explore humanity and the worlds we are creating at the same time. What better journey is there? To live intensely in a world and create another world simultaneously. Unheard of! Ridiculous! Wonder!

This rule helps allow us to release the need for things to turn out a certain way, which, in art, makes a lot of sense. We're creating something with passion, and passion can be . . . messy, unpredictable, uncontrollable. We're also staying open to the unexpected, like where our characters might take *us*, rather than what we should do with them. Rather than maintaining something rigid, like even a very helpful outline, sometimes we must deviate, and that choice is an important one.

Ultimately, we will find balance between free-flowing stream of consciousness and rigid structure. For some of us, it takes a little work to learn to let go of our envisioned outcome, but when we do, we will be able to dig deeper than we ever expected.

Once we release ourselves from the idea of how things should be, we can relax and simply create. We're going to play a little now with visualizing things to life.

#makingreality

QUICK TIP: Let It Flow

As you move through these games, thoughts will come to you while you are writing. Don't bat them down or go back and forth in your mind about whether that's a word you should include or not. You are working in a new way, and when you start resisting these thoughts, it's pulling you out of the present. Moments are passing you by. Like meditation, just notice you're doing that and let go of the thought that wants you to change your idea or that judges your idea. Continue creating in the now. It's all going to be okay, because in improv, there are no mistakes.

GAME: Pick an object, any object!

We're going to use our imagination to write about a random object for a few minutes.

WHY ON EARTH WOULD WE DO THIS?

If you've read the Pulitzer Prize–winning *Goldfinch* by Donna Tartt (if you haven't—SPOILER ALERT!—skip ahead quickly to the next set of instructions), you'll know that the entire book is about a painting and a young man's journey with it and relationship to it. If an object and the description of an object and a few of its "owners" (it's stolen) can hold us spellbound for over five hundred pages, there's something to objects and our obsessions with them. They can take us on a journey we never could have planned.

- Set the timer for three minutes
- Choose a number from 1 through 100.
- Select the corresponding number from the Objects list in the appendix on page 195.
- Visualize the object.
- Write about the object, describing it and perhaps its owner, until the timer goes off.

Nice job!

QUICK TIP: No Planning, Structuring, or Expectations

Let's release the desire to plan anything! This will help with being in the present moment, the next rule. Going with the flow helps with the rest of the rules here and, really, with all of life.

WARM-UP: Classic Object Work

Now we're going to get a little bit physical by creating an object out of thin air. Actually, the very same object you just wrote about. It became real to you in your mind; now you'll make it real with your hands.

You may feel silly at first; that's natural, and you're not alone, especially not the first time. But by the end, you'll be more comfortable pulling and shaping an imaginary and very malleable clay. It's easy to work with, but take your time to form the details, the creases, the lines, envisioning your object becoming a solid thing.

WHY ON EARTH WOULD WE DO THIS?

Using an imaginary mound of clay, we see and feel an imaginary lump become a real thing, just like our stories. This one sentence doesn't come close to capturing the breakthroughs I've seen and felt after years of doing object work. You make this thing up onstage, and people are talking about how *real* it was days, years later. It's not nothin', if you know what I mean. It's making something from nothing.

- Set the timer for sixty seconds.
- Visualize a lump of clay or Play-Doh in front of you.
- Using only your hands, start stretching the imaginary material in front of you to create the shape of the object you wrote about in the Pick an Object game.
- See it, make it.

Good job!

GAME: Making a Monologue

Continuing to build on this, we're now going to write about—or as—the object that we have just spent some time making real to ourselves (and to anyone watching through the window).

If in your game you found a knitted hat with cat ears, you can become the cat-hat and tell the story of how you ended up on the beach, or the park bench, kid's room, wherever you are. If you found a crumpled letter on the forest floor with blood on it, perhaps you write the letter or tell the story of the person who wrote it or found it.

WHY ON EARTH WOULD WE DO THIS?

The main way actors bring stories to life is in their portrayal of very specific characters with very real mannerisms, movements, manner of speaking, and so on that fit within the world like a glove. It is the same for writers. When the actor is committed to the character, there is a freedom to create that arrives on magical wings. Suddenly everything that happens is right. It is the same when we write, committed to the character. And in this game you are committing to being a "character"—either a person or inanimate object with a specific point of view.

In improv, what you come up with just is what it is. It's not a cookie-cutter, "we have to do it this way" process. The freedom is glorious. Please partake. But have no expectations that any certain kind of quality, form, style, or story will emerge. You will find that you surprise yourself.

Write a series of these in a certain style or with objects that are complementary, and you might have a monologue-type book, a series, a collection of one-act plays or poems, or. . . .

- Set the timer for five minutes.
- Write a monologue from the point of view of the owner of this object, the object itself, or as a character coming upon this out-of-place object.

- As the owner of this object, perhaps you want to talk about other things too. . . .
- If inspired, keep going after the timer goes off.

Good job!

EXAMPLE

I selected "Arrow" randomly from the list.

Arrow.
I am air. I am speed.
I am infinite misery.
With no aim, I am harmless.
Targeted, death.
I was whittled
From the strongest tree in the forest
I will not let you down.
I have been shaped, molded, fitted
With the sharpest blaze of iron found
In future or past
I am the one thing standing between
Your hatred and your destiny
Your hunger and a bountiful season.
Choose me from amongst my brothers.
Light me with fire.
Your desire will not be denied.
I am strong. I will not split in two.
I will make my mark and you will not forget me.
You will not leave me behind
In the tree
That I came from.
I will bring the mighty to their knees.
The weak to their graves.
Do not pass me by this time.

Rule #4: Trust

In improv the philosophy is, there are no mistakes. When you trust that there are no mistakes, you are off the hook. No one is watching you, grading you, judging you—not even you! Everything is as it should be in the moment. Some savvy writers who are super focused on the structure of storytelling might think this isn't important, but I view this belief as a hyperrelevant quality-of-life kind of choice—to decide that what you come up with and, equally important, what your partner (or editor) comes up with is not a mistake. Whew! Suddenly I can relax.

I hear you. "Wait, wha?! You mean I don't have to be perfect?! Hold your hairy eyeball here, Harriet! Let me make sure I'm getting this. Because I used to get hit on the knuckles for making a mistake. Are you sure?"

In writing, as in life, we get blocked and frustrated when we are holding on too hard, too determined with our outcome, too set in our ways to adjust to what is happening around us. Seeking perfection. We become unable to see and feel and write the possible gifts that abound when we don't set ourselves free to explore and try and possibly fail. So what if we do fail? There are a million memes and coaches and inspirational books out there to remind us that the trying is the important part; the journey,

Since it turns out there are no mistakes—not in improv, anyway—we are free. And since writing, really, is *all* improvised, when you get down to it, your writing is also free. The vitriol we wouldn't ever aim at anyone else, yet we aim at ourselves and our own work from time to time, is free to dissipate. And in its place is pure creativity for the sake of creativity. Because we are our often our own worst critics, we can also decide to just finally let go.

not the destination; and so on and so forth. In fact, the "freedom to fail" movement is having a bit of a moment. Many people are agreeing this is a good time to get out there and make an attempt. You've seen them, heard them, read them; now it's time to practice it yourself. Here. With a free-spirited heart.

Don't get me wrong; I know ritual and planning and logistics are good and important and have their place in our lives. I'm just suggesting that if we loosen the reins a little, let our imagination take flight, have faith in ourselves and our ability to create something powerful, we can accomplish more than if we stay the course and create only what we had envisioned when we set out. If, instead, we follow the signs, get into the flow, be ready to adjust, we might just find ourselves doing a whole lot more than we ever intended or expected. We just might surprise ourselves knowing that everything you create when you play is okay.

Trust your words.

For example, some pretty serious inventions were actually documented, verifiable MISTAKES. Look 'em up! Alexander Fleming discovering penicillin. Wilson Greatbatch's implantable pacemaker. Spencer Silver's Post-it Notes. Naval engineer Richard James's Slinky! Ruth Wakefield's chocolate chip cookies! What are you waiting for? Join

Thomas Edison and the Dyson (vacuum) dude and get to failing, going wrong, veering off the path. Brilliance awaits.

In school, one of my favorite classes was art. I liked the part where I sat down with an empty page or canvas and started to fill it. That was the best! I had some idea of something—a building, an object, a something in the corner suggesting a start. But unless it was an assignment of something specific given in class, when I was arting for art's sake, I would always start with that idea and then let my hand go and draw or paint what it wanted. I followed nothing too too closely, too too consciously. And somehow, I guess through doing a lot of improv, I have maintained that attitude with most things, as much as I can. Certainly, I've done so with my characters onstage or on the page. That's what I am asking you to do. Free it all up. Let the goose on the loose. Have some fun. Play. Don't expect to be winning awards and accolades. But don't be surprised when you do.

Because a free, full-of-faith heart, connected and really in the trenches of life, creating and empathizing and sharing and being open and vulnerable and transparent and not really caring all that much if anybody looks or sounds silly or what others will think—well, that heart can't help but win. At life. And either way—any way—we're trying, so we're already winning. And we can trust that.

#youknowwhatswhat

GAME: Freeform Writing as an Object

Yes. You read that right! You're going to be an inanimate object and write from its point of view!

WHY ON EARTH WOULD WE DO THIS?

Doing this exercise helps to build a little trust in yourself that you can improvise, creating off-the-cuff work in a playful way.

This exercise helps to release the need for things to turn out a certain way. It moves you into the realm of allowing for new ideas to come in—without worrying that it's a mistake or headed in the wrong direction.

In writing for animation, I've found I enjoy writing from an inanimate object's point of view. Just like I do in improv, playing a chair or a spoon and bringing their point of view to life is one of my favorite things to do. If you're not used to this, or this seems strange, try it out. You may just find a perspective you never would have otherwise.

Once we release ourselves from the idea of how things *should* be, we can relax and simply create and then trust that it all will somehow work out, because it always does.

For example, if you write WWII historical fiction, write about or *as* a German Mauser rifle or a life vest. Yes, we're playing games, but you can also tailor improvisation—that's really the whole point. I'm giving prompts, but it's *your* imagination. Feel free to choose your own object, I am certain you'll never look at said object the same way again after deciding to become the object and writing in first person—er, first object.

- Choose a number from 1 through 100.
- Find your number in the Objects list, page 195. You can also use an item you would find in the preceding exercise, where you fully created your environment.
- Set the timer for five minutes.
- Visualize the object. (If you chose from the list and don't actually know what the object is, spend a couple of minutes looking

it up to understand it. Don't research something you already know about the first time you play—just go ahead and play!)

- Become this item.

- Write from the point of view of the object. Perhaps you focus on letting it tell its history, where it's meant to go, who owns it, and so on.

- Now play again, this time spending a few minutes researching the object. Do an image search. Check out early versions of it or who invented it; go deeper on your second time playing. That goes for all the games!

Good job!

QUICK TIP: Relax

We do simple warm-ups to settle our minds and find a calm, focused place to be for the purpose of listening. You can also achieve this in one quick step: relax. Let go of that tension in your neck and shoulders. Take a deep breath and release. Go on, love!

When you interrupt, you've stopped listening.
People need to be heard.
—JERRY SEINFELD

5

Rule #5: Listen

Listening is a form of observation. And observation is the whole wellspring of stand-up comedy. "What's with the....?" Just an observation. If we can really be present in life for the big moments and the small, we will catch it all, or as much as catch can. Writers are often unusually smart, I think, because they are simply aware enough of what is going on around them: being present, then observing, absorbing the world through the senses in a heightened state of awareness and then filtering it through their very unique program so that we can enjoy the result.

Becoming a great listener is a gift to yourself and everyone around you. When you can listen actively to your own intuition, you can keep yourself out of trouble or imminent danger and make decisions you are confident in moving forward with—in your writing and in life. When you can listen actively to the world around you, you can hear the beauty of the wind rustling the trees, the teeming city life that will be starring in your next story, the silence that makes the sounds pop. When you can listen to others actively, you can have real relationships. For the page, listening actively to others means really understanding the people around you, really understanding your characters.

When we really listen to the big moments and the small, we catch much more of what's happening around us. This also means it is important to listen to our characters and our own creative, constructive voice.

#listeningislove

QUICK TIP: When You Talk, Focus on Who Is in Front of You

In improv, our main focus should always be on our partner. When we do this, a magical thing happens: we're taken away from looking at ourselves and what we're doing, how we appear, what people might think about us; instead, we're laser-focused on, curious about, caring greatly about, and daring greatly with our scene partner. If you write with someone, try applying this same principle and see how it shifts the dynamics of your working relationships. Try it in conversation and see how it shifts your social life too. When we're writing alone, our scene partners can be our characters. If we've put in even a teeny bit of work and understand them a smidge, we can listen to them the same way. We already do this, anyway. Now we can listen to them with purpose and intention, and honor them as though they were standing in front of us. When we do, we get the same reprieve from self-consciousness. On your next pass through your story, you can focus entirely on another character in your story. In this way, each gets alone time with you and dimensions that they didn't have before.

GAME: Set It Up!

We're going to plant ourselves in a place we've never been before and absorb all that we can through our imagination and our very real earholes.

WHY ON EARTH WOULD WE DO THIS?

Let's step beyond ourselves into observing every moment. Let's start listening to our characters, our own inner voice, and everything else we can tap into. Let's invite it all in so that we can mix it up, stir the pots, and deliver something unheard of to the world.

Great listener, great writer.

You can create a file of all the pages you come up with, settings, protagonists, and so on. You may find they are usable right now for a project you are on or that you will revisit them later.

- Set the timer for ten minutes.
- Choose a number from 1 through 50.
- Find your number in the Settings list, page 201.
- Write the setting at the top of your blank page.
- Plant yourself in this environment. Look around the joint.
- Let your imagination take over.
- Listen, listen.
- Write what you hear. Write about the sounds. Let it spill over into what you see if that's what happens naturally.
- Keep writing, keep listening until the timer goes off.
- Look at this lushness. You're flush.

Good job!

GAME: Character Visit

We are going to play now, in character. And we are going to hear sounds as this person and write about them, all while in character, all by simply selecting a protagonist to be and putting the character in the place you just wrote about in Set It Up!

WHY ON EARTH WOULD WE DO THIS?

What a joy it is to begin regularly practicing (if you don't already) fully immersing yourself in your character, seeing and hearing as them, discovering the world in a new way. And when you're done, you'll have brought a slice of it back for all of us. Yes!

- Set the timer for three minutes.
- Choose a number from 1 through 100.
- Find your character in the Protagonists list, page 198, choose a character you have been working on, or create a character who would live in the setting you wrote about in Set It Up!
- Write the name of the protagonist at the top of the page.
- Plant the character in the environment you just wrote about.
- Listen, listen.
- As your protagonist, write what they hear. Write about the sounds and what it makes them think of—a memory, a dream, just observing?
- Keep writing, keep listening until the timer goes off.
- If you have more to say (or your character does), set the timer for another increment of your choice.
- If you're feeling inspired, play again in another environment. If you'd like to write as the character in their own environment also, try that too. These games are now yours to use to develop your characters, your worlds, your imagination.

Good job!

> You always have two choices:
> your commitment versus your fear.
> —SAMMY DAVIS JR.

Rule #6: Commit

I touched on the following point earlier, but I learned this in teaching: say something enough times, and eventually one child listens. Please hear my drumbeat on this. It's a huge part of why I wanted to share all this with you, because it is has saved me over and over and over from humiliation and self-hatred. People often comment on my willingness to get up after being knocked down—and believe me, as a sole female stand-up comic on most shows, out there espousing my political and personal beliefs, this happened, a *lot*. That knocked-down thing. But I kept getting up. You wanna know the secret to that? I was safe, truly, baby-wrapped-in-a-favorite-blanket safe. And there's one reason I was safe. *Commitment.* I was safe from the audience if they didn't laugh, other comics (and we can be a mean bunch), and most importantly, safe from myself.

Safe from yourself, you ask? But maybe you don't ask—because you know too well how mean we can be to ourselves, our looks, our ideas. No one is safe from self-hatred. And it's a very dangerous game. Save yourself and learn one of the quickest ways to slay that devilish dragon. I say devilish dragon because what's scarier than a devil? Right? And what's scarier than a dragon? Exactly. Don't let those devilish dragons tell you your idea is not worthy, that you are not a person with writing ability, that you should binge more content with a bag of chips—no! Do not do this. Do. Not.

Instead, commit. Commit like your life depends upon it. Because it does. Remember the devilish dragon. He's just chillin'. But that won't matter once your skin is so thick from committing to yourself and your creation time. It won't matter what editors and reviewers and in-laws say. You'll know, in your heart, that you gave it everything you had.

I'm trying hard here to translate what committed, confident performers enshroud themselves in before the camera rolls or the curtain opens, so that you can have it too. It's like a veil, light as bridal lace but strong as chain mail. It's this DECISION to move into the forward time-space continuum, giving everything you have inside yourself over to the character. It's losing yourself in the world you are creating, fully disappearing, the way you did as a child in your favorite fable.

I want to help writers who are hard on themselves, or critical of their own work, to develop a magnificent shell of strength and confidence that cannot be cracked by executives, dismissive family members, agents, or trolls. It ain't easy, and it takes some work, but the following exercises are variations of those that have transformed students who walked in a little hunched into ones who walk out with their chests puffed out and a twinkle in their eyes.

Martha Graham said

There is a vitality, a life force, an energy, a quickening that is translated through you into action, and because there is only one of you in all of time, this expression is unique. And if you block it, it will never exist through any other medium and it will be lost. The world will not have it. It is not your business to determine how good it is nor how valuable nor how it compares with other expressions. It is your business to keep it yours clearly and directly, to keep the channel open. You do not even have to believe in yourself or your work. You have to keep yourself open and aware to the urges that motivate you. Keep the channel open.

Sometimes when people think about improv, they think: Head over to Crazytown. Get wacky. But the good stuff is grounded. Even if you're a can of soup talking to the can opener, it can be from a real place. A place with heart and soul. With meaning. Pixar has shown us that.

This is home base for me. Graham was a work of art herself—and what beautiful permission she gives us here. All we have to do is commit to doing it and doing it 110 percent. Which of course makes no mathematical sense, but art isn't measurable, so let's say 110 percent. Because we know what that means. It means extra effort, extra commitment, and then extra return. Give and you get.

Commitment to what? Commitment to character, to the scene, to simply deciding to be someone who can do this. Commitment to being a frog in a scene with a lizard. It never mattered to me. If I did this one thing: Decided. To. Be. Then I was safe. If I did this one thing with absolutely everything that I had—like a horse with blinders on, like a madwoman with no other option, like a maze-running mouse focused on the cheese—I could get something done. I could create an effect, I could survive the challenge, I could . . . I could . . . I could be anything. That is the point I want to drive home. We have so many options, so many desires. All we have to do is pick one thing and commit to that like the world is ending, like it's the only thing that matters, like we're made of molecules that could just disappear. And guess what? From this sweaty, steely, focused decision, we can accomplish what we set out to do.

Maybe it's finally listening when our characters speak to us. Maybe it's letting go of the notion we aren't good enough. Maybe it's just setting a timer for twenty minutes and not budging from the chair until it goes off. (Oh, excuse me; mine just went off.) Commitment will save you from critics, self-criticism, and danger, every single time. I promise.

There is a way to become a confident artist without being a narcissistic egomaniac. To become an artist who knows that they have intrinsic value, as well as something valuable to offer: their own unique viewpoint, the way they think about things and the way their individual imagination puts them together. Commitment teaches us this. And I think that having confidence in yourself is directly proportional to finding appreciation in others' work. I want to be *very* clear about this. I think the strength in one's self-confidence has a lot to do with having appreciation of others' creations. Of *not* being critical of others. And it is possible to lessen the critiquing of everyone else, subtly—or obviously. I have felt this and observed students realizing it.

As I mentioned earlier, providing information onstage in improv is sometimes called "gifting." Why? Because it takes the pressure off the other performer standing onstage. It's hard to be judging yourself, when you're caring for others. Step outside of yourself and give to your characters. Let *them* be judge-y of each other, but you don't need it. There's already enough of it from agents, reviewers, YouTube, and so on. . . . Ugh.

I have observed that it is more difficult for some of us to let go of criticizing than it is for others. So much of what we do comes down to our thoughts. I mean, we're writers, right? Where do our words come from? Our ideas; our thoughts. The same thing that can help us write compelling characters and addictive stories (our ability to switch into our characters so deeply that we are thinking the way they do) can halt our continuous onslaught of shoveling scoop after scoop of hatred onto ourselves and others. What's that thing? Changing the way we think.

One of the best ways I have found to change how I think is to discover, learn, and absorb the mightily different narratives of others.

There's an ancient Chinese proverb that sums it up:

Be careful of your thoughts, for your thoughts become your words.

Be careful of your words, for your words become your actions.

Be careful of your actions, for your actions become your habits.

Be careful of your habits, for your habits become your character.

Be careful of your character, for your character becomes your destiny.

If Publius Syrus's observation that "When we speak evil of others, we generally condemn ourselves" is true, then I believe the opposite is equally true: when we speak well of others, we can be kinder to ourselves. That is what I am inviting you to do here. That is what great improvisors do. They include the other people onstage; they don't exclude them. They add to the suggestions presented in the scene; they do not negate them, correct them, or make the other character smaller (unless they are specifically playing a jerk of a character; then all bets are off, and the game is afoot). Great improvisors *give* of themselves continuously and within split seconds. This means the thoughts of such a person are already geared toward making others look good, enhancing a moment, embellishing what is already there, not trying to drag everyone with them in a new direction/sinking ship. This takes courage.

Courage is something Brené Brown has researched and written about for years. In *Daring Greatly*, she writes with great insight about people using criticism. Especially as a shield. "It doesn't matter if your great dare is politics or the PTO, or if your great dare is an article for your school newsletter, a promotion, or selling a piece of pottery on Etsy—you're going to be on the receiving end of some cynicism and criticism before it's over. Why? Because cynicism and criticism, cruelty, and cool are even better than armor—they can be fashioned into weapons that not only keep vulnerability at a distance but also

Don't think. Just move.

can inflict injury on the people who are being vulnerable and making us uncomfortable."

Sometimes your words will make people uncomfortable. I hope so. That's part of what we do in creating tension and storytelling. But maybe it's you or your subject matter that get to people. So what? Your voice, and your using it, are the whole point. It's your angle; it's why you matter. But please don't get wrapped up in your worth coming from people liking or not liking your work. I think I've done that enough to last me the rest of my life. I'm gonna listen to Brené Brown regarding my worth, criticism, and finding the courage to dare—and I hope you do too.

Commitment is the secret key to unlocking the cages of criticism so many of us have found ourselves in or built around ourselves.

This is work for the long haul. It's not a quick fix, but fortunately, it's simple. You will soon discover the power you are capable of wielding when you use this rule. The first step is to not think too much. In improvisational theater, we say, "Don't think. Just move."

Here's a challenge for you.

#iamcommittedtoyou

GAME: Committed to Character

Become another person and let them tell their story. I believe you can do this, because you just became a character who owned an object *and* you became that object in an environment you wrote about. Bam! You did it! Now let's do it for just a little longer, go a little deeper.

WHY ON EARTH WOULD WE DO THIS?

Oh! This is the stuff. In a cursory way, we are getting additional insight into a new character, which is kinda profound. But it does go deep. With practice of this exercise—and really any improv games focusing on character—you become talented at switching the voices, the characters in your brain, so that your dialogue is natural and the characters have a separation. You can go as deep into a character as you want to just by making the decision to put everything you have into seeing the world through their eyes, living as them, and bring that richness to your work. I urge you to commit to the character (like no one is watching—cuz guess what? no one is!) and see for yourself.

- Set the timer for three minutes.
- Choose a number from 1 through 100.
- Find your number in the Protagonists list, page 198.
- Write about this person you've randomly selected. Just make a list of twenty to thirty words that describe this person: emotions, physical strengths or weaknesses, personality traits, and so on. (If you get stumped, there are lists for all of these included in the back.) Go ahead write and create until you have a pretty good idea of who they are—maybe you can even visualize them physically. Just try to write about them until you understand them to some degree. Take more time if you need it.
- Reset the timer for five minutes.
- Right there in your chair, become this person you've created,

and write in the first person as them. Even if you don't normally write in the first person, give it a shot.

- Write until the timer goes off.

Nicely played!

WARM-UP: Movement in Character

We're going to take things a step further. A literal step. Farther. With the same character. On your feet. You can do this. Many schools teach this as a warm-up; it's great to start getting into the body of different characters.

WHY ON EARTH WOULD WE DO THIS?

As writers, we can control things pretty well. We make a lot of decisions that affect our character, and this exercise gives us a chance to give up control and let the character have some. And as I mentioned earlier, practicing doing this enables us to see and then write through many different sets of eyes, giving us unlimited access to all the characters we create. As we'll see later, these simple improvised exercises can be used on all characters. No more one-dimensional princesses. Not on your watch.

- Set the timer for thirty seconds.
- As the character that you just worked on or one of your own that you want to explore further or you are more comfortable with, get up from your desk and embody that character.
- Just stand as they would stand; if they get curious and want to move a little, go for it! It's all good.
- If you're on a roll, try it all again with another character for a full minute!

Good job!

GAME: Character Shoes

Get ready; we're going on a walk . . . as another person! Wait, what?

WHY ON EARTH WOULD WE DO THIS?

After years of working in the theater, I found that sometimes I didn't really have the character until I had the right shoes on. When I changed my clothes and stepped onstage, in full costume, with the completed set, everything shifted. I know we're not going that far here, but this is one of the main reasons I feel so compelled to share these games and the performance aspect with you—because there's gold in them thar hills!

This adds onto the first exercises, allowing discovery about your character with a short trip around town. I'll admit, this takes some amount of bravery, but I believe in you! You get to practice seeing the world through the character's eyes, living as this other person for a more extended period, possibly even interacting with a cashier or a stranger.

- Put on a pair of shoes—specifically, shoes like what your character would wear. Get as close as possible to what you think this person might wear.

- As the character that we just worked on or one of your own that you want to explore further (farther!) or you are more comfortable with, go on a short walk as them.

- That's right, head out the door. No timer necessary.

- If you want an additional challenge, go in somewhere, buy a pack of gum, or order a coffee to go.

Well, hello! Look at you!

> If the environment permits it, anyone can
> learn whatever he chooses to learn; and if the
> individual permits it, the environment will teach
> him everything it has to teach. "Talent" or "lack
> of talent" have little to do with it.
> —VIOLA SPOLIN

Rule #7: **Be an Expert**

Just as the value of visualization for athletes has been proven, there is scientific proof that deciding you want to be something makes transformation easier to achieve. I ask you to live as your characters many times throughout this book. In this chapter, I ask you to trust that you are your characters and write as them, first on a topic that your character would be an expert in, then again for a few minutes on a topic they wouldn't normally know a lot about.

The best way to do good work is to first *believe that you are* going to do good work, great work, or whatever you want to call it. There is a fun game in improv called Expert; I've played and taught it and seen it performed in a variety of media. The person, the *character*, is being interviewed, and the audience has assigned them a subject on which they are now suddenly and thoroughly an expert. It's terrifying. After doing it a few times, you learn that merely *deciding* to be an expert is, in some ways, a gain in knowledge, in and of itself. Yes, I am suggesting you *can* just decide to be whatever kind of creative person you dream of being—and be that person. If you aren't already. This is like what I learned from emotions (which we'll get to in more depth later): that you can have control over them. And your thoughts, too! I learned this from an improv game and from my mom. Oh, and it's a blast to practice. Then you apply the Commit rule, and you are in it to win it!

To follow this rule, we must first decide that we are all brilliant writers. Then we must decide that our character is a complete expert in that field. We let our characters inform us; we become the recipient of their genius. We don't have to be geniuses ourselves; the pressure is off. By playing, acting out, *becoming* our lead characters, we may learn new information, choose a new angle from which we want to write. And you don't even have to perform onstage, leave your home, or do anything other people would look at you oddly for. No one needs to know you're someone else, an expert on [fill in the blank].

This requires commitment to being in character for a longer period, but the payoff is pretty great. You'll choose a character you are working on or select a person you know well. You can also, after a time or two, move on to an advanced version and select a character—from the list in the back of the book or your own—whom perhaps you don't understand very well and want to get to know, or a new one you're developing. Ideally, you'll return to this game repeatedly to mine the gold. In sketch comedy writing, some of our strongest characters are based on our mothers or that wacky character we see every week in group therapy. Whomever you choose, just make sure, the very first time you play this, that you have at least a grasp of the person or character. When we play this game in class with young kids, I must make sure that children have heard of and have some sense of the characters we're making them—they figure out who they are based on the clues we've given them. Children *love* this game, and I hope you do too.

If you choose a character from a current project, before you answer, make the decision to be the character you're working on. Sit as she would, hold the pencil as he would—just *be* this character and commence answering. There are no wrong answers.

Then set the timer and, as that character, fill out a simple questionnaire to reveal their beliefs, values, and knowledge. This process reveals a lot of information that will offer you a new understanding of whomever you are "playing."

As you play this game over and over on lead, supporting, any, and all characters, know that improv games are for everyone. I've been adjusting and changing the games for years to suit my students' needs, and you can too. Make up questions that are more pertinent than the ones I've provided or deal more directly with the uniqueness of your character's world. I've included broad questions that I would ask someone during a professional interview or on a date, to get some sense of what they believe in. Writing novels is nearly the only art form that allows someone else to really know the thoughts of a character. You can be inside someone else's thoughts for three hundred pages. That's a lot of inner monologue. And this game offers a chance to practice going deeper into the mind of someone else, if you give yourself the freedom of knowing that nothing you come up with in these writing sessions is wrong. And none of it is wasted time. It's not just backstory. It's a deep exploration of the essence of another human being you will introduce the world to. And you can be as good at being them as you are at being yourself. That's improvisation. Acting. And you can do it right there at your desk. Shall we?

#officiallyanexpert

GAME: Press Conference

You'll be a random person answering many questions with confidence. This improv game has been around for decades, and today *you* will be the expert.

WHY ON EARTH WOULD WE DO THIS?

I'm going out on a limb here. As with the other exercises, you'll gain more insight, a heightened level of commitment, and ultimately more confidence in your own ability to transform and therefore find the interesting things about each character you're creating that you can write about.

I know there are a lot of backstory creation exercises, but I don't know of too many that ask you to commit to the idea that you already know the answers and just let them unfold. And that whatever you come up with, in that moment, as that character, is right. All this work is right, because it's that character answering, not you. So the most important step is committing to be the expert, to becoming this person. If you struggle with this, or any of the exercises, it's okay. We're working creative muscles and imagination. Sometimes when you're working out, you pull a muscle. You wouldn't get great results without pushing a little. I say, push harder.

- Fill yourself up with confidence. Firmly commit to doing this exercise—to being an expert.
- Choose a character you are working, select a person you know well, or choose a number from 1 through 100 and find it in the Protagonists list, page 198.
- Decide that the character is an expert at being who they are.
- Set the timer for ten minutes.
- Become the character.
- As the character, answer the questions—some of them taken from actual journalists interviewing figures in history—in the Press Conference Questions list, page 198.

- If you played the first round as a character you already know, play another round with a character chosen from the list! Write a few of your own questions on the second round, getting more specific and asking the tougher questions.

Howdy, expert!

QUICK TIP: Write with a Partner

If you have a writing partner (or you can grab a buddy from your writer's group), try playing Press Conference live! When one person is committed, they can answer like any important figure at a press conference: honestly, with heart, like a child, off on a rant, lying, antagonizing the journalist, and so on. Have fun, stay committed, support each other!

In displaying the psychology of your characters,
minute particulars are essential. God save us
from vague generalizations!
—ANTON CHEKHOV

Rule #8: Be Specific

Comedy people know you can often get a laugh or really catch someone's ear by getting specific. Why say, "She's at that hotel down the street" when you can say, "She's at that fleabag circus house downtown with the trained monkeys at the door"? I'm going broad, as I like to do, but that's my taste. At least give us a "He sauntered into the refurbished Park Avenue hotel" instead of "he went into the hotel."

The scenes actors paint on the stage in improvisation come to life with the addition of detail. When a description (whether verbally stated through dialogue or as an aside to the audience or even demonstrated through pantomime) is shared using adjectives—the bells and whistles of storytelling—the audience can suddenly see what the characters see: the lush forest; the dingy basement; the lost, sullen boy in the corner. This is the magic of telling stories.

This game is a tool to begin practicing adding as much detail as possible—to color in the world you are creating. This will help to clarify your own thought process, and it will also help the story come alive for future readers. Eventually every detail in your story will be pertinent to the character and world, but for now, splash the color—let turquoise and magenta tinged rainbows fly.

#itsinthedetails

GAME: Five Objects

You'll be making a list, quick, quick, quick. No thinking.

WHY ON EARTH WOULD WE DO THIS?

This first layer here is pointedly about not thinking, about letting your brain roll information forward. We'll stop that "stopping" train in its tracks. Go ahead, just let your creative caboose loose. Remember to work as fast you can.

- Set the timer for thirty seconds.
- As quickly as you can think of them, jot down five objects you would find in a *museum's basement*. Go!
- Keep in mind, there's no wrong answer, we're going for speed here—don't think!
- Feel free to play again using the Settings list, page 201 or the Settings (Made-Up) list, page 202.

Good job!

EXAMPLE

Given the suggestion of a grandmother's purse, what might you find?

1. Tangerine
2. Rubber band
3. Toothpick
4. Pair of glasses
5. Envelope opener

GAME: Five Objects and One Random Item

Let's play it again, Sam, but let's also level up. I think you can handle it!

Get specific with each item you write down. *Annnd*, make one of them something that is random, that you wouldn't normally find there.

WHY ON EARTH WOULD WE DO THIS?

To mine for comedy, the unusual, the absurd; to surprise ourselves in unexpected, interesting stories that can be unearthed. In my classes, I always let there be an oddball answer. Because in life, sometimes you find syringes on beaches. I know, right?

- Choose a number from 1 through 50.
- Find your number in the Settings list, page 201 or a create a setting of your own.
- Set the timer for thirty seconds.
- Jot down a list of four things you would find in that place and *one* thing that doesn't belong there or would be a surprise if it showed up. And . . . maybe there's a story there. In fact, if you're excited about this, set the timer for a coupla minutes and come up with a little more material. Even just the start of a story. Ready, set, GO!
- Feel free to play again by choosing a number from 1 through 30 and finding it in the Settings (Made-Up) list, page 202.

Wow! Look what you did!

EXAMPLE

If you are finding objects on the moon, maybe one of them is a Rolex watch with a shattered face.

GAME: It's Not Just . . .

"It's not just a _____ ; it's a _____ , _____ "

Add some details to this Mad Libs lookin' game to create a very specific kind of object or person.

WHY ON EARTH WOULD WE DO THIS?

We can see for ourselves how a story about a tricycle suggests itself in the example for this game, which follows the instructions. And with imagination, we can find out what happened to its owner, or who stole it, or . . . the possibilities are endless. It's a creative person we can start to build a scene, a story, a life around. The traits that an object or character have can hint at unseen imperfections and idiosyncrasies—the things that can lead to character and story arcs. The devil is in the details!

- Choose a number from 1 through 101.
- Find your number in the Objects list, page 195.
- Set the timer for ten seconds.
- Describe it further. It's not just a _____ ; it's a _____ , _____
- Repeat, resetting the timer and playing with a new object from the list, until you're beating your own time. No thinking!
- It's not just a _____ ; it's a _____ , _____
- It's not just a _____ ; it's a _____ , _____
- It's not just a _____ ; it's a _____ , _____
- Set the timer for five minutes and write about—or *as*—one object that catches your fancy.

Good job!

EXAMPLE

It's not just a tricycle; it's a broken, rusty tricycle.

GAME: Five Objects—All Very Specific

Now let's practice listing items and building more and more descriptive words on top!

What kind of tangerine? A squishy, over-ripe tangerine.

What kind of rubber band? A broken, gray rubber band.

What kind of toothpick? A used, tea tree oil–flavored toothpick with some gunk on the end. *Ew!*

What kind of glasses? A pair of orange-framed glasses with the bridge taped together in the middle.

What kind of envelope opener? A porcelain envelope opener with blood on it.

WHY ON EARTH WOULD WE DO THIS?

We're building more muscles here. Muscles of *not* thinking. Huh? That's right. We're getting faster with creating and putting on the page, so we're not thinking AND we're coming up with interesting things!

We're really getting into the start of a possible portrait here. I think that in any five descriptive objects, we can start to pull out a character, even get some creative vibes on the setting containing these objects. The point is, anything that is included in our pieces can be more specific. When we start to go there, we are not just Painting the Scenery (an upcoming technique in which we'll use objects like the ones just listed to create an environment); we are allowing ourselves to see it too. And when we are living *inside* instead of outside our creation, whole other ideas, points of view, angles, barriers, directions, possibilities just show up.

- Set the timer for twenty seconds.

- List five things that can be found in a high school principal's desk drawer. (Notice you have less time to do this—that's because I believe you're getting quicker.)

- Reset the timer for thirty seconds.

- Write down five things you would find in a high school principal's desk drawer—but with objects that are very specific, like we did in the previous exercise. It's not just a _____ ; it's a

  _____ , _____.

- Play again and randomly choose a number from the Settings list or use a setting of your own.

- Repeeeeeat!

You clever creature!

EXAMPLE

If you are finding objects on the beach, maybe in the first round, one of the items is "a beach ball." By the second round, you are coming up with things like "a discarded, grimy, half-filled syringe" or maybe "a red, white, and blue surfboard with shark tooth imprints."

QUICK TIP: Don't Make Things a Joke

In improv, we are guided by "don't *try* to be funny." We are trained to let the funny come out of the characters, the game, the situation. So don't bother trying to come up with witty words—at least at the beginning stages. (If, later, you want to write with the witty hilarity of P. G. Wodehouse, be my guest! That might even be your style. I would never hold you back. I just don't want you getting hung up.) Let your words reveal the funny through a grounded reality, even if you're writing fantasy, high drama, or a tragedy. Trust yourself that the funny will arrive at the right time.

> A gift consists not in what is done or given, but
> in the intention of the giver or doer.
> —SENECA

9

Rule #9: Set an Intention

I can't tell you how many times I have had a much better time performing, bowling, cooking, or doing anything really, when I set an intention. Maybe it's applying one of the first several rules: be present, listen, commit to everything or have fun, or have fun committing to everything. Make up your own rules! I dunncare! Choosing just one thing to put my energy into works for me. If someone asks me later whether I did what I set out to do, I love to respond. My improv teammates and I do that after shows. Because we tell each other before we even start what we are individually going to focus on during the show. This is different from No Expectations, because you aren't planning what will happen, but rather deciding that you will put extra effort into one creative aspect. "I'm going to support the other people onstage at all times." "I'm going to try out some new characters, since that scares me." "I'm going to let my criticism monster have the day off and not judge a single thing." What is your intention with what you are working on now? If you've never set one before, I invite you to now.

Stick the landing

Setting an intention can help strengthen any weak spots you may have. Maybe it's focus? So you decide to set the intention of writing with focus. A timer and a program to turn off the interwebs can help with this, but nothing will be stronger than you deciding you will do it.

In this warm-up, you will come up with a list of specific intentions. This list focuses on the aspects of writing and preparing to write that you would like to strengthen or buff up. Feel free to work on one each day, on repeat, until you are masters of them all. Then make another list.

#designyourowndestiny

WARM-UP: Readying Ritual

You can decide before you start writing how you want your session to go, how many words or what kind of writing or whatever it is you would like to have happen for the next coupla hours.

WHY ON EARTH WOULD WE DO THIS?

This little moment we take for ourselves can have a huge effect on our work, and we discover bit by bit, decision by decision, intention by intention, that we are the masters of our own fate. When we decide something *will* happen, the chance that it will increases exponentially. Rituals have been around for eons, and what makes them work is the setting of an intention. The decision is important. So, yeah. Whatcha want?

- Create your own prewriting ritual, such us lighting a candle and listing your goals for that particular writing session or setting a timer or putting on a certain kind of music.

- You can write it on a card to remind you before you dive in.

Nice!

After my morning meditation, I look over what I will be writing, get a sense of where I want my writing to take me, and make a decision about how far I want to go and any problems I want to solve. I bring a giant jar of water with me. You know, for the journey.

Today, I am grateful for the space to write and the interesting journey my characters take me on. I light this candle to remind me the illumination of imagination burns brightly. Before I am done, I will have written three thousand words. I will end my day on a satisfactory note and have resolved this whole "how do they meet" conundrum.

Now we're going to spend just a couple of minutes focusing ourselves. Even a wonderful scene onstage that seems to come out of nowhere began with someone deciding to _____ [fill in the blank]. I often try to focus on listening or being present, because I figure some good stuff can come from that, and even if it's not fireworks, I was at least in the room for it.

GAME: Choose Your Own Intention

Now let's map out a little bit. I know, improv is so not about planning, but what we're looking at is what you want to do within improv.

WHY ON EARTH WOULD WE DO THIS?

We're writers, and when we write something down it has more juice, more power, more intention. So, aside from making the decision of what kind of writing session you want to have, why not go bigger and really put it out there, where you can see your dream, consciously and subconsciously, every day? Let me know when it happens!

- Make a list of intentions you'd like to work on *over time*. You should be starting to get used to writing fast and not thinking by now, so get ten or twelve things down without thinking about it too much.

- Riddle me this: which three call to you, make your heart sing?
- Write them on a piece of paper or an index card.
- Tape it to your computer or in front of wherever you write.
- Change each one out for a new one once they start happening!

Hooray for the day!

QUICK TIP: Intend to Enjoy Yourself

Especially if you are writing comedy, discover what is fun to write about. If you don't know what's funny to you, start a dedicated note-book—your own Comedy Observation Notebook—and keep it with you for a week. Write down everything you laugh at. At the end of the week, your funny bone will be more exposed to you (and others) than usual. Then get back to the games with the intention of having fun, and see how there is a correlation—that the more fun you are having, the funnier your characters in their situations get.

> I wonder how many people, whatever their medium, appreciate the gift of improvisation. It's your one opportunity in life to be completely free, with no responsibilities and no consequences. You don't have to be good or even interesting. It's you alone, with no one watching or judging.
>
> —TWYLA THARP

Rule #10: Judge Not

How, you may be wondering, does criticism fit into the creative sphere? It does not. Not at first, not in the beginning with that seed of an idea. Let it be yours to grow into a mighty oak.

As I mentioned earlier in the book, there is a correlation between the extent to which we commit—to a character, to our work—and our ability to not let criticism affect us. I'm excited for you to discover that the more fun you have, the less you will feel the need to criticize your own work.

According to Del Close, the dude who basically brought improv into the pop culture zeitgeist, judging has no real place in the creation phase. Close clearly states not to judge unless it's about entering (think new characters entering a scene you're working on) or cutting. Aha! Cutting. And when do we do that? Not until much later. As writers, we shouldn't be doing any cutting while we're writing. Editing is a phase meant for later, as a different person: as the writer/editor person, not as the writer/creator of worlds-n-stuff person. No, no, my friend. NOT: "Well, that's a stupid line. How cliché." Only strategizing, like "Should I bring step-sister Shelby back into the scene, so they can have their big fight now?" See the difference?

Many great and successful artists have a lot to say on the subject. Twyla Tharp talks about criticism being unnecessary in her creation. So did Mozart. He said: "I pay no attention whatever to anybody's praise or blame. I simply follow my own feelings." And this is exactly what an improvisor onstage must do, what I invite you to do. Follow your feelings. Let the scene, the story, the characters you love and create take you beyond judgment.

Let us relax. Let us not care so much about what others think or even what we think ourselves, and let's just get down to the business of being a creative machine. Let's try a new way of looking at our art and habits and take a chance on trying new ways to come up with ideas and stories.

Deciding to give up judgment gives us freedom, room for a playful attitude, and space for more joie de vivre. Improvising also means no judgment. There simply isn't time for it. And if you expect to get back up onstage and reveal all the humiliating, wonderful, sassy, ugly, next-to-naked, and sometimes even naked for real (I've seen it and I'm not suggesting anyone do it, I'm just saying I've seen it) sides of you, then you cannot be judging. You simply don't have the time, space, or inclination if you're really creating in the moment. You cannot be judging—not yourself, your partner, your work, the last line, the next line, the audience, bananas, nothing. Nothing.

Please don't evaluate your work while you're in it. And best not to even bother with that afterward either. Editing is different from criticizing. Let's make a homemade quilt. A safety blanket. You're never too old for one—at least not if we're talking about creating with the same freedom we had as kids.

Now cast a vast empty thought, a blanket, around and above you to be free to create within. And *within* is key here. If we can get inside our creation—be the characters, live in the world we're the architects of—then it's easier to let go of judgment, because we are using our spirit of play from childhood, where we're just doing it, we're in it. We don't need to stand above the sand castle and point out the crooked turrets, the broken moat; no, we have to save the dragon and get the king and queen to safety. There's no time! Critical thoughts have no use, no purpose in the general throes of creativity. Critical thoughts create a stop and start that maybe gets some things polished and pristine, but as a whole? I believe we're losing organic possibilities that can take us beyond. Just beyond. How many times have we heard that a great song was written within a few minutes; the writer just let it flow, and out it came. We know that doesn't happen with everything—sometimes there's tinkering to do—but, in general, with a first draft, a first pass, please treat it as an actor would a rehearsal. Give it as much as you would a performance, stay in character, and commit 110 percent even though the math makes no sense, until the director calls cut.

Even if there are mistakes. A professional actor doesn't stop a stage rehearsal and say, "I stumbled on my line; can we go back a pentameter?" No, he plows forward. How many times are you going to go over this ground in the future? Plenty, so for now, please think like an actor, at least in that sense, as you go through these exercises. Allow the emotions to boil and thunder and the imaginary world you are simultaneously the architect of to become real to you. Very real indeed. Be in it. Not above it.

There's only one game I'm going to ask you to play right now, and it might be one of the most important. Would you consider being really kind to yourself while working through these games? Like you are a soft, sweet puppy with big eyes, just learning how to go after a tennis ball? Would you play the game of being kind and good to yourself while you try working in a new way? To agree to get it out there, to get something started, not judge it as good or bad or anything at all? Just don't do it. More about that later—and help with getting rid of the inner critic—when we discuss criticism, but for now, it's all good. And not as in *I'm judging things to be good*. I'm saying: It's okay. It's all okay. Fine. Yes. Okay. Good. Good work. I can't wait to see what you and your imaginary improv team come up with!

Now we're going to play a couple of games designed to work on building a certain kind of feeling that improvisors who have many shows under their belts naturally accumulate at show's end. A simple, triumphant kind of "Huh. Well. I did that thing." Some lucky few are able to walk away from auditions and performances without wishing they had said a line differently, played the scene differently, chosen a different character. Others cry in their car after an audition or literally bang their heads against walls wishing they had made different choices. I know which one I would rather be. Following are a couple of games you could roll your eyes at, but guess what? Sometimes it's the simple mechanisms that work the best.

#behappywithwhatyouhave

GAME: The Glad Game

In this game, inspired by the classic novel *Pollyanna*, we're going to consciously find things that we appreciate about strangers.

WHY ON EARTH WOULD WE DO THIS?

This game is centered on appreciating the people around you while you develop this skill. I do believe it is a skill, and that it, like a watered sapling in the sun, will grow big and tall and strong. This is a gift to others and to yourself. It may seem simple, but after years in NYC of playing this on the subway when I felt myself start to hate the crunch of other bodies near me, the intensity of so many people, this one little game made me fall in love with eight million people all over again, just like the day I showed up there, big-eyed and naïve. Give it a shot. It truly connects, lifts, and gifts.

By usurping Pollyanna's Glad Game from the eponymous book (and movie), you can begin to practice admiration and appreciation for the people and things in your environment, which leads to feeling more connected and less critical. All because you found something worthy of gratitude? How can this possibly work? Well, it doesn't come so easily to all of us—it takes effort. But not too much—here's a two-step process that can be done daily, with phenomenal results.

In fact, if you made this your writing prompt for the next 365 days, you'd develop some interesting characters with this one game alone. Here's your challenge:

- Head out into a public place, a café or a stroll around your neighborhood.

- Find something you like. Notice it and consider why you like it.

- Find something else.

- Find something you like about the person across from you, wherever you are.

- Find something you like about that other person near you. Each person has a certain aesthetic sense; you have yours: something that makes you glad, makes you smile in even some small way.

- Find another something to appreciate about someone. Their shoes perhaps? Shirt?

- Go until you find yourself smiling and feeling a little more connected to others—this is a great place to start improvising from.

Wow! Nice job.

QUICK TIP: Opposite Day!

The opposite of criticism is appreciation. So whenever you feel yourself judging others, start looking for things to like. Whenever you are getting down on yourself, remind yourself of something cool about you. It's Opposite Day!

GAME: Diary Entry—Glad Game Subject

Now, we will take it another step and take that person you found
something to like about and write a short diary entry for them.

WHY ON EARTH WOULD WE DO THIS?

We're doing this exercise to reduce judgment to create a feeling
of "like."

I believe this is the path to creating more realistic antagonists, letting go of the mustache-twirling villain and leaving in his wake a
human being with thoughts, feelings, dreams. What will you write
when you write in this person's diary as them? That's up to them, isn't
it? Because you are no longer holding the strings. You are no longer
puppeteering; you are leaving room for someone you judged, albeit
briefly, to tell you who they are. And in this small way, you can let
go of judging yourself, because it's not even you anymore is it? It's
a new friend or, in some cases, an excellent new adversarial foe for
your story.

Working with Pollyanna's Glad Game reminds us of the power of
gratitude and is the biggest weapon I've found outside of criticism
to slay the inner critic. When Pollyanna really needed it, she was able
to put her game into action and change the downward trajectory
of her life. The Glad Game can help anyone get out of a self-critical
thought pattern. It also helps in adjusting expectations—better yet,
consider having none.

- Imagine that this person you have admired in some way has
  a journal they write in, and write an entry as that person: first
  person, committing to the character, and letting the world
  unfold to you through their eyes.

- If it was an inanimate object, like a purse with peacock feathers
  that caught your eye, write the entry from the point of view of
  the purse. Or the owner of the purse. Or the peacock.

Fantastic!

Bonus Rule:

Conjure Enthusiasm

Okay, this isn't really a rule, per se; rather, it's encouragement from me based on years of teaching kids who were never bored, and if they were, it wasn't for long. If we're not into what we're doing, no matter the task or project or experience, it just doesn't have the same vibrational force. If you aren't into it, either *get* yourself into it or pick something else to play at, because you aren't doing anyone else any favors laboring away on something that not only isn't fun but will eventually suck your soul up like a handy dandy patented Dyson.

For example, you're working on a story, but you've either lost passion or you never had it. Well. You've got two options as I see it and have seen it with students. One: You change course and pick a different subject, one that lights you up and keeps you lit all through the night. Two: You find a way to get pumped. You stumble upon a kernel of research you were unaware of; you come at the thing from a new angle like a sniper/ninja/jungle cat; you just GET PUMPED!

The only true barrier I have found throughout my years of teaching is a lack of interest. Again, this isn't a classic rule but a result of standing in the classroom or theater for years looking into the eager (and the not so eager) faces. I think most teachers can agree. Without engagement, it's like staring into that empty vacuum tube. No power. Endless boring days. This bonus rule is also here because I know what it's like to write on a show that I'm hired to do but not inspired by. I admit that some of the ideas I have come up with for my own passion project have been completely without passion, and I didn't realize it at first. So I include these exercises to do double duty—to save you time by (1) keeping you from writing on projects you're not intensely inspired by and (2) helping you find inspiration. Writing doesn't have to be a slog. I know it is for some people. But it doesn't need to be for you.

find your passion project.

Instead, focus laser-like on the things that matter, the subjects you are about. Find a way to get enthusiastic about what you are working on. I discovered that doing this with my stand-up on the nights and weekends made my money job endurable. Creating without the passion? Nada! Even that sentence looks sad. Creating without the passion. Like it shouldn't be allowed to exist. . . .

I want to break the word down for a second. I do love etymology. And "enthusiasm" is one of the coolest. Per Merriam-Webster, "enthusiasm" comes from the Greek word *enthousiasmos*, from *entheos*. Possessed by a god, inspired. Or divine inspiration.

How cooool is that? This is all open to a little interpretation, but are you getting where this is going?

It was originally two words put together: *en* and *theos*.

For you lovers of Latin out there—you know who you are, you *amantes*—yes, you know that *theos* in Latin is "god." *En* is "in." "In god?" Wha? But you *amantes* also know that in the Latin languages, many words are in another order. Which would make the root of "enthusiasm" "god in."

Do you see? When you are enthusiastic, god is in you, part of you. Of course you can translate this to be a higher power or whatever quality you want to equate to a power, a force, a feeling. I'm using the root of the word here, but I want this to be open to your interpretation and how that directly relates to your writing, your art. What the Latin language and I are trying to say is, if you can get yourself to a place where you are enthusiastic, it will catch on and affect others like nothing else in this world. It will be divine.

Let's dip into your dream projects.

#focusonfun

GAME: Springs on the Soles of Your Feets!

We must find the things, the projects that help us leap—yes, leap—out of bed in the morning. It is possible, but sometimes it takes a little digging, a little effort to turn the pursuit into play, something we can't wait to do.

Here is a quick game to help you narrow your focus on projects (if that's sometimes an issue for you) or help you find a new one if you're seeking that.

WHY ON EARTH WOULD WE DO THIS?

Without enthusiasm, it is very difficult to consume information, do exercises, play, or create. When we tap into something that brings excitement and passion—something that makes us feel like we're revved up—we can work in depth for extended periods of time, and be truly happy with the results, even if it's a first draft.

You can come back to your lists and add to them repeatedly as you explore and produce material on the things that interest you. This is a way to keep your writing fresh and to keep yourself interested. This is a very important piece of your work and one that improvisors naturally do onstage, without thinking about it. Why don't they think about it? Because there isn't time. You just go to the next thing on your mind, and usually it's a character that you like, that inspires you, that you can have fun with in some way. Why shouldn't all writers be reminded of that from time to time? In improv, so many really fun and funny characters just show up. Sometimes they're weird or they have hair in strange places or they are super-villains. Let yourself explore, and let these new characters surprise you—I really think they will.

Ask yourself, "When I go to a bookstore or library, which three or four sections do I hit up first?" Make a short list of these on an index card.

- Put these on your computer or in front of where you write.
- Choose a number from 1 through 50.
- Find your number in the Settings list, page 201.
- Jot that setting down.
- Set the timer for two minutes.
- Envision the setting.
- Decide on a character to be from your short list. (If history is a go-to for you when you're browsing books, you might become Amelia Earhart, Napoleon, Marie Curie, or their like.)
- Imagine yourself as this character; be as committed as any actor onstage could ever be. Begin writing either a diary entry, a letter to someone the character cares deeply about, or a simple story the character is writing from life. Write as this character in this place—if it is strange to the character, that might be exactly what this person wants to discuss. No rules. Just discovery.

Great!

EXAMPLE

I am drawn to the history section, also the YA section, or I check out the latest picture books—so I jot down young adult, children's, or history books. Then I set the timer. I imagine myself passing through hundreds of nonfiction books, letting my mind sift through them—or, if I'm struggling, actually going to the library or even doing a search online. (Don't worry; you can start the timer in the aisle at the library, but you'd better have your notepad, because I think and hope for you that the ideas will be swirling.)

I settle on a woman I remembered reading about who had started a particular orphanage. I start thinking about the time she lived in—what it was like to run a home for children in that era, who would have helped her and who would have stood in her way. I immediately have two additional characters. Tone pops up in my mind (without my thinking about it), and I know I want it to be less grim than anything I've ever seen before. And I start to take this real story far, far away into a world that I've never seen before. In my monologue, I begin to flesh out this young, single woman, trying like mad to do good in the world. I think about her. About what she looks like physically. I find my lead has a deformity. It brings up even more obstacles. Especially in this time period when little would be known about what she was dealing with, day to day. And with every obstacle that starts to pop up, the more that is thrown in her way, the stronger she starts to feel to me. She is becoming real. And so is her right-hand girl, a teenager herself, who arrives to help her on this journey to creating a safe haven. But perhaps she isn't who we think she is. . . .

Presto—a new start of a story in under five minutes, any and every time I want it! I might include another random character or two characters from this world. I can do this every day and rotate through different sections of the library, depending on my mood or interests, and always have a new character, setting, premise spinning. There is an absolute abundance of material to draw from. It's much like how you experience those terrifying few seconds of walking out onstage in front of people with no idea of what you are going to say, but then a talking zebra shows up or an armchair or a grandmother who settled on the plains. I use this short list all the time. And then I expand it. As if I could ever tire of talking teacups.

WHEN YOU WATCH A DOCUMENTARY, WHAT SUBJECTS ARE YOU DRAWN TO?

- Producers of documentaries must be passionate about their subjects; sometimes they spend years, even decades, researching and filming them. As if you were setting out to make a film, select *your* subject. Something you care about.

- Set your timer for five minutes.
- Outline ten to twenty important moments in this event or in this person's life.
- Decide what angle you would take.

look at that!

WHEN YOU WERE A CHILD, WHAT WERE YOUR FAVORITE BOOKS?

- Set the timer for ten minutes.
- Begin listing the stories you connected with the most.
- Go back and reread the list. Write a few sentences, at least, on why each one impacted you.
- If you were not a big reader, you can add some movies to the list!

Great!

WHEN YOU CHOOSE A MOVIE TO WATCH, WHAT ARE YOUR FAVORITE GENRES? WHAT DRAWS YOU TO THOSE CHARACTERS?

- Set the timer for five minutes.
- Write out the answers to the questions just posed.
- Select someone from your life who inspires you and whose presence makes you *enthusiastic*.
- Reset the timer for five minutes. Without thinking about it at all, write as them. It could be a letter, inner thoughts, a rant, etc.
- Look over your favorite genres and select one that this person would fit into. Maybe not comfortably, but they could exist as a certain type of character in the genre.
- Reset the timer for five minutes. (I know! This is a juicy one. Get in there!)

- Put them in a very uncomfortable situation within this genre. (Choose a number from 1 through 50 and find it in the Premises list, page 196.)

Good work!

My friend Diane inspires me. There are so many cool things about her, I don't even know where to begin. I'm going to create a character description of someone (inspired by Diane), and she's going to be the best friend in my next rom-com. Because everyone needs a friend like her, with her great advice—which the constantly losing-herself lead, Kayla, really needs to heed, but keeps resisting. Maybe I can make it more active by putting Kayla in a dunk tank at the carnival; every time she disagrees, Diane hits the mark, and the lead gets a good dunk. Suddenly I really want to write that movie.

GAME: Passion Player

If you were thrown onstage, what kind of character would you be most comfortable playing?

If this freaks you out, calm thyself. You don't have to go out there. But, imagine if you had to. Like, people were waiting and your lead has food poisoning and there's no other choice. . . . C'mon, who would it be? What kind of person? Not a real character from history—unless it's yours.

WHY ON EARTH WOULD WE DO THIS?

The more symbiotic and connected you are with a character, the easier it is to write from their viewpoint. To tell their story. If you're not comfortable becoming your characters while you write, this is a way to ease into it. If you *are* comfortable, take the opportunity to get outside your comfort zone: if you're always writing dangerous heroines, for example, go in another direction, once again opening yourself up to further possibilities.

- **Pick just one for now. (You can always come back and do this again with your other made-up pals.)**
- **Set the timer for three minutes.**
- **Write a short piece on this sort of character and why you are most comfortable with him or her.**
- **Set the timer for another three minutes.**
- **Be the character and let them write about what they *love*—what lights them up.**

Great job!

EXAMPLE

I'll share mine. When I go onstage, my go-tos and enjoyment are playing animals (talkative animals), kids, aliens, and inanimate objects. Surprised that I write cartoons? Me toooooooo.

QUICK TIP: A Date with Inspiration

If you are ever looking for inspiration, I am going to recommend taking a page out of Julia Cameron's book (hey, not literally!) and taking yourself on an Artist's Date. I still do this. You have to make your own list, but I'll share four of my most favorite things to do: Go to a museum. Take a walk in the woods and sit and listen to the leaves in the trees. Go to my favorite bookstores. Head out to the vintage shops in search of treasure. What are yours?

GAME: Mining Magazines

We're going to take another turn and play one of my favorite games for coming up with a character and/or a setting. We're going to select an image of a person from a magazine and then discover who this person really is—beyond the split-second snap decision that we might initially make. You will now likely pay extra attention the next time you find yourself at a magazine rack (I know I do—mining for unusual magazines to write a character around), but until then, here are some categories (for more actual titles, see the Magazines list, page 194).

Animals and Pets, Antiques and Collectibles, Art and Photography, Auto and Crafts, Cycles, Food and Beverage, Health and Fitness, History, Hobbies, Home and Gardening, Men's, Music, News and Politics, Parenting, Psychology, Religion, Science and Nature, Sports and Recreation, Teen, and Women's.

If you don't have access to buy the hold-in-your-hand copy, check them out online—there seems to be a niche magazine for everything. (Check the library too; most have vast current collections.) Print a pic of someone or some*thing* (if you're like me and like to write for animation or as an inanimate object).

Here are some specific worlds you can select from. Who would be the people who read—or write expert contributions to—these publications?

Architectural Digest, Car & Driver, Family Handyman, National Geographic, Popular Science, Real Simple, Rolling Stone, Southern Living, TIME, Vogue

And here are some more unusual (but real) mags:

Berlin Quarterly, Boat, Cereal, Dirty Furniture, Ladybeard, Mold Magazine

I'm getting ideas for characters, just reading these titles, and I hope you are too.

WHY ON EARTH WOULD WE DO THIS?

The visual image gives us a specific place to work from. And when we delve into understanding a human whom we had judged only by their looks, once we've gotten to know them, we discover how much more there is to them.

So we're coming at specific characters who exist in these worlds, or are maybe the opposite and very uncomfortable in these worlds, or are dealing with someone therein. There's a *Vogue* magazine just for children, called *Vogue Bambini* in Italy. Think about that one—the chichi mom who reads that to dress her daughter like a runway baby! My head spins at all the possibilities for characters. Just the collection of children's magazines being published in the world alone can send you down a rabbit hole of ideas for animated films or family films. Or just creating an interesting character in any story. All the new possibilities can really get you excited!

You can even treat this game like an assignment to write an article that you wouldn't have pitched but had assigned to you, for which you are getting paid handsomely. In other words, you can also treat this as an exercise in finding a way to connect to and find enthusiasm about *any* subject. You just might find yourself surprised by how much your character fancies cats, working on a pic from *Cat Fancy*, even if you're more of a dog person.

Part of what we're doing here, also, is breaking out of our routine, not just to find things we're enthusiastic about, but a new way of working, creating, *playing* that is like the word "enthusiasm." Possessed by the above. The gods, if you will. Or God. Your call, but stir those feelings and let them grow wild and burble.

- Go to your local magazine store or wherever there is a collection with dozens and dozens of options. We want some choices. (Or turn to the Magazines list, page 194.)
- Select a magazine *you* wouldn't buy, but that interests you in some way. Maybe it makes you laugh. Or think. Or it's just that weird.
- Buy it (or look at the website).
- Look through for a photo of someone that catches your eye.
- Cut that person out (or print a photo of them) and set them in front of you.

- Set the timer for five minutes.

- With the knowledge of Rule 7 "Be an Expert," become this person.

- Write as this person—maybe they are writing in to the magazine, maybe they are writing in their journal, maybe it's just a stream of consciousness (as them) on their love or hate of something. . . .

- Bonus version: Repeat the game and mine another character. Do all the same steps. Then put these two in a scene together, choose a number from 1 through 50 and find it in the Premises list, page 196, and see where it takes you!

Good job!

EXAMPLE

One student brought in *Cat Fancy* and created a lovable cat-grooming character I couldn't quite get out of my mind. This ended up being a character she created a monologue with and dazzled all of us with how it came to be, how funny it was—but also grounded in reality.

Someone else brought in a quilters' magazine and created this character that had nothing to do with the picture you might have had in your mind just now about what a person who reads this magazine was like (turns out there are several choices for great, real, creative people to discover and add to a project or base a story around, in *Quilter's World*, *The Quilter Magazine*, *Quilter's Home Magazine*, and more). Made me think. Just like in life, people are never just as you imagine they might be if you are only *looking* at them. Get in there. And be amazed by what you find in their minds. By the way, I think this is the coolest thing about acting. When you're in it, you have all these thoughts and ideas that aren't yours. Freaky at first. But that's exactly what we're aiming for here. Transformation. Getting lost in our writing and coming out the other side going, "Whoa! I had no idea, when I chose this image, *this* is who that person is." This is the exciting power of the combination of your imagination and commitment to character.

QUICK TIP: Game of the Scene

In improv we often refer to the "game" of the scene. It's defined in many ways by many different performers and programs, but mostly it has to do with what is unique about the scene, what is interesting and catches us, so we're like—wait, did that just happen? In a comedic scene it's often the first thing the audience starts laughing at, and the players bandy it about like a cat with their catnip-filled toy mouse. Watch out for unique things to pop up. Instead of deleting them, see where else they can take you.

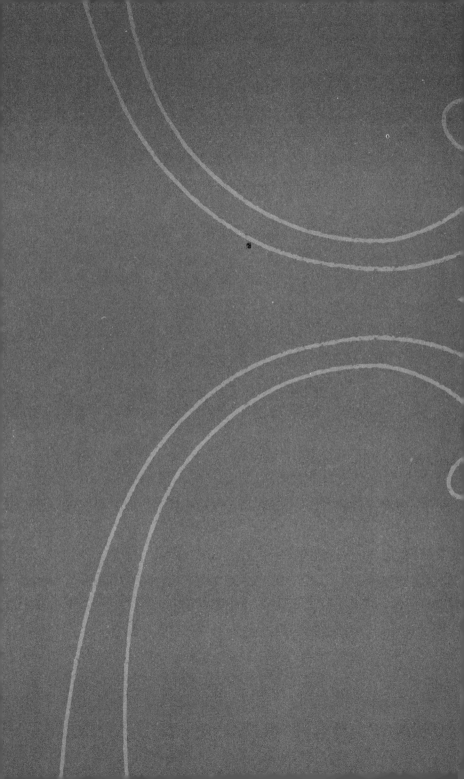

PART TWO

Applying Improvisation to Story Elements

> Ideas come from everything.
> —ALFRED HITCHCOCK

12

Ideas

Remember, you are an idea machine! Yes, you are! And you can come up with infinite story ideas in a millisecond, with some Jedi mind training. Which is what we are doing. See what I did there? YES. AND. And also, you're a Jedi!

Today and every day going forward, you can just know you are capable of coming up with ideas like a well-oiled mechanism; they can just shoot out of you! Ting! There goes another one. Tang! Hey! Watch where you're pointing that!

It's your job in life to think up the wondrous, the fabulous, the magnificent, the dark, the wild, the whatever you prefer. Why? you ask. Why are you tasked with this? Because! You can! You have been chosen. By yourself, by a teacher in third grade, by something bigger, but it's you. You're the one making up everything, dreaming it all, building walls. And I am just here to give you another tool, method, means of continuing the path you were never supposed to get off of.

You can plug any of these games into you—the idea machine—and within seconds you will have something. How do I know this? Because I trust you. And I believe in you. And the world needs your ideas. Not because we're running out. Because there's a place for you. A place for you to make your mark. And all you need is . . .

IDEAS.

There are a lot of definitions for the word. I like the Merriam-Webster one you have to dig for a little.

Idea: "an indefinite or unformed conception."

Something, some thought, character possibility, place, nebulous thing is conceived. And importantly, it is malleable. It isn't something that has all the pieces in place yet. What a great place to be sitting pretty.

Now of course, eventually your story idea will become more focused around a character who needs to grow in some way—and who does so by traveling through a particular plot or set of circumstances/obstacles. That's for later! Now's just for letting any and every germ of an idea fly. Woooo hooo! Feel the freedom!

Every story everywhere exists because of an idea. But where do they come from? Where can we get them? As you know, they truly are everywhere. Sometimes when you are in the most private places, on a solo walk in nature, in your morning pages, in the shower, on the bus, standing in front of the coffeemaker, wading in a stream fly-fishing—they just—poof!

But guess what? You don't always have to wait. You can jump-start your own idea machine into existence. These exercises can help you tap into more story ideas if that's what you are needing *right* now or at any point in your creative career. I hope to get your brain wheeling and dealing so fast, your face can't keep up with it. That's right.

Generating ideas is one of those things that a lot of writers struggle with. Even if writers have plenty of ideas, so many say that the hardest part is to just start. In improv, someone just pulls you onstage sometimes, creating a feeling like jumping out of an airplane and then expecting *you* to come up with ideas! What? *You* pulled me onto the stage—I thought *you* had an idea. Why are your hands so sweaty? And sometimes you go onstage because someone must do something, even if you don't have an idea yet, and you somehow come up with something in the six steps from the back wall to the front of the stage. You do it. It appears to be magic, but you have incredible tools to pull from in that split second.

This next exercise is me pulling you out onstage and you imploring to the heavens above: "Wait, I don't have an idea!" There have been times I've just had to trust that some idea was going to get channeled into my brain and come out of my mouth. And guess what? Not once did I or any of my students stand and stare at the audience and humiliate themselves. Because an idea always arrived and saved our hides. I believe the same thing will happen for you now, if you believe too.

#itsallgood

EXERCISE: Ask for It

It's infinite, the answers you can emerge with over the years, just by practicing listening. I'm not suggesting I know where the answers come from. From me? From something bigger? I'm just so excited I went "fishing," as David Lynch would say.

I've learned from teaching that everyone learns differently. I've learned from strangers that everyone has a story. And I've learned that when looking for answers, we get them from different places. But let's see if there are some out there floating about, waiting for the chance to join our in, pending, or outbox projects.

WHY ON EARTH WOULD WE DO THIS?

What does this even have to do with improv? A bit, actually. As I mentioned, I have stood onstage, in the back line, *needing*, oh desperately needing, an idea to come to me. When you are onstage with the knowledge that your teammates need you, they want you to step forward and create a transition—I mean, they just got the biggest laugh of their scene, for goodness sake; feel that rhythm, get out there! It is time to go, go, go! But. One big problem: I had NO IDEA. Not one. But my feet stepped forward. I did NOT, for the record, ask them to. But they stepped forward, the idealess rest of me went along with it, and on the way to the front of the stage, I was sent an idea. I think because I asked. So . . . ask?

I've gotten so many incredible, fun, wonderful ideas when I took the time to ask for them and receive them.

- Sitting comfortably, set the timer. Choose a time that seems doable for you. Five minutes would feel short for some. Some writers I've heard say they go for ten minutes. Maybe you need two? It's not as important, the length today, as that you make time to return to this exercise to fill your well, especially if this is working for you and yields results.

- Close your eyes and settle.

- Focus on your breath.

- Perhaps do some counting of the inhale, the exhale.

- Then let that go and try one of these two things:

  - Open to receive thoughts and let them come and go, not focusing on anything, and see if anything comes to mind. If it's like lightning—and occasionally it is—be sure to jot that down.

  - Ask a related question. I like to ask, "What do I need to know today?" or "What story can I tell?"

Well played, sir, ma'am.

You are an idea machine.

GAME: Family Portraits

This next game is ignited by a visual. I mean, we can't sit around all day asking for ideas and not getting any and getting annoyed. (By the way, if that happened, it ain't no thing but a chicken wing. Try it again some other time, but for now, check this out.)

We're going to come up with some ideas—malleable ideas, remember! That takes the pressure off. And we're going to use some silly images, or not so silly, if you look up the Romanovs. You'll see.

WHY ON EARTH WOULD WE DO THIS?

This is a game meant to do three things—mix up our routine, get us to write quickly without thinking, and possibly give us a subject to build a story around, using characters who catch our eye. By the end, you'll have several new ideas for characters, settings, world-building, and so on to put in projects, write in-depth about, or lock in the attic for later.

- Do an internet image search for "family portraits."
- Feel free to refine the search, depending on interests, to "weird family pictures" or "surreal family portraits" or "holiday portraits gone wrong"! Inspiration will chase YOU after a little time spent searching on keywords like "awkward store Santa portraits"—or swap in "Easter Bunny" for "Santa."
- Pick one out that makes you laugh or think—one you have a strong reaction to. Just be careful not to fall down the rabbit hole—too far.
- Set your timer for three minutes per character.
- Start writing out a character description for each person.
- Then write out their relationships to each other.
- Include how they feel about themselves—and how they feel about the others in the picture.
- Reveal what they want to do in the world outside of their family.
- Get as in-depth as you want to.

Noyce work!

GAME: Your Local Library (Never Be at a Loss for Ideas Again)

My favorite library ever is the New York Public Library. I would spend hours upon days there, crawling through the stacks (maybe actually crawling—don't judge me. Remember that rule? Heh!), finding new characters, writing, writing again, researching. Most of the categories listed here are from the Library of Congress's Classification System. Fancy, right? They are ours, and this is a chance to really make use of this institution. I use this library to come up with ideas for short stories, characters, settings, specific episode ideas, you name it. It's a resource for all of us, and after you use it on these games and others, it will start to become second nature and you will be able to come up with ideas in a split second. Just like improv! I have included broad and niche library categories here—you will find you are drawn to some of the same subjects repeatedly over time.

WHY ON EARTH WOULD WE DO THIS?

So I'm going to offer this exercise, and you can start out all chillaxed and easy-does-it style, by picking out a few settings that you've never written about or even thought much about, to jump-start some creative new ideas. Then if the story gets intense and you are really surging forward, go to the actual library and spend time in this section and do the research and back up that scene with even more confidence in this new setting for your story. See where that takes you. Who knows? Maybe you're paid to write a lot of mysteries, and suddenly you're in a historical fiction land firing everyone up with your wildest imaginations, imaginating everywhere.

- Head into your library. (If you can't make it to the library, I also have a list compiled in the back of the book—most of them categories from my beloved New York Public Library. Have at it!)

- Get a library card—did I really write that? I mean, get the library card you've possessed for years and use regularly. Ahem. Okay, digression over. (But seriously, support your local library if you're lucky enough to have one! I can't imagine life without one.)

- Go to three sections that interest you.

- From each, pull out a couple of books that grab your attention.

- Narrow down your selections to a couple that, when you look through, you can feel your imagination kick-starting itself.

- Check them out of the library.

- Tell the nice staffer at checkout that you're a writer and you're doing research for your next project. Isn't that cool?

- Take them home and review; choose one subject and one location within that subject.

- Now create a character from whatever world you've been looking into with these books.

- Imagine this person and try to picture them.

- Set your timer for five minutes.

- Write about this person, looking at them from the outside, anything one could observe from looking at them or knowing a little about them.

- Reset your timer for five minutes.

- Now write as that character, taking on their view of the world and life. Write what it's like to be them or about what is important to them.

- If you're in the middle of a thought when the timer goes off, keep writing; you don't have to put the pen down if you're inspired.

Good job!

EXAMPLE

I like philosophy. I might choose that and then, specifically, Aristotle's favorite bench. Then I would choose Aristotle, since I chose his bench. And without looking anything up, just going off my knowledge of his life and teachings, I set the timer and begin. I'm just describing what I see: robes, sandals, and so on, but also the expression on his face. Then for the next step, I write about what he's planning to do that day, because my mind right now is curious what Aristotle's to-do list might look like!

GAME: Your Local Bookstore

This variation on Your Local Library might just blow your mind. When I think about this too much, too long, my head starts imploding and exploding at the same time, which is, as you might imagine, an odd sensation. Dangerous. Provocative. Okay, let us go shopping! When you are in the bookstore, there are all these sections, right? Aisles, areas with area rugs, shelves with their own brackets. So many pages delineating life for us, giving a collective bank of infinite ideas, inspiring, educating, elevating. I am so excited I can't hardly wordsies. You must take over! Go, my new friend! Create!

I went into my favorite independent local bookstore and started jotting down the sections for your journeying into the unknown pleasures. Here's what I came up with from a bookstore (you'll see a lot of crossover with the Library Sections list, page 193, but there are plenty of differences too).

Action-Adventure, Animals, Antiques and Collectibles, Architecture, Art, Biography, Business, Children's, Cinema, Classics Fairy Tales, Computers, Cooking, Crafts, Crime, Detective, Dolls and Puppets, Economics, Education, Environment, Family, Fantasy, Fiction, Fitness, Foreign Language, Gardening, Ghost, Graphic Novels, Historical Fiction, History, Holidays, Law, Literature, Mathematics, Medical, Music, Mystery, Mythology, Nature, Performing Arts, Pets, Philosophy, Photography, Poetry, Political Science, Psychology, Relationships, Religion, Science, Science Fiction, Self-Help, Social Science, Sports, Technology, Television, Toys, Transportation, Travel, True Crime, Thrillers, War and Military, Westerns, Young Adult, and more!

I included a few that were subcategories, but I couldn't help myself. When I saw Dolls and Puppets, a million animated show ideas and kids' projects leapt out at me.

WHY ON EARTH WOULD WE DO THIS?

This is going to yield an unlimited array of possible directions in which you can take your story. I'm not saying go look to other books for ideas; I'm saying look to these divisions of interest to spark ideas for settings, characters, world-building. A plethora of possibilities.

I hope you love it as much as I do, because I feel that through studying improv and spending time in my favorite places (libraries and bookstores), with their powers combined, I have the keys to the kingdom.

I like playing bookstore in the same way that I liked playing banker when I was a kid. Didn't you also lend your parents money when they were broke and had to stretch to pay day? I really love this game because when I need an idea, all I have to do is close my eyes and land in the shop, walk down the aisles, let my fingers trail along the shelves, and wherever they stop: next scene. Maybe it will stay in the story; maybe it's just something to get the wheels turning. Please keep in mind, each of these areas has subcategories. What? Do you do what I do, always go to your go-tos? What are the sections of the bookstore that you are always writing from or within? Maybe we can deepen it by exploring the subcategories within the overall. If you were looking to write another great sports story and you wanted to go deeper than your last awesome baseball story that you sold, let your mind dip into the possibilities on the shelf. Here is an example taken from the sports and recreation section of my favorite bookstore in LA.

Air Sports, Archery, Basketball, Boating, Bodybuilding, Bowling, Boxing, Camping, Canoeing, Cricket, CrossFit, Cycling, Equestrian, Field Sports, Figure Skating, Fishing, Football, Golf, Gymnastics, Hiking, History of Sports, Hockey, Horse Racing, Hunting, Juggling (what?), Kayaking (okay, we're back on track. . . .), Lacrosse, Martial Arts, Motor Sports (hmmmm. . . .), Mountaineering, Olympics, Polo, Pool-Billiards (huh?), Racquetball, Roller and In-Line

Not everyone's imagination is sparked the same way, of course. You might like sitting in the woods doing some forest bathing (OMG please try this!), or researching real people in person, or looking through visual images in print or film. Be on the lookout for new ways of getting inspired.

Skating, Rugby, Running, Sailing, Scuba and Snorkeling, Shooting, Skateboarding, Skiing, Soccer, Speed Skating, Sports Psychology (what a cool angle—I'd love to see that movie!), Squash, Swimming, Table Tennis, Track and Field, Training, Triathlon (I'm tired just thinking about that one. . . .), Volleyball, Walking, Water Sports, Weight Training, Winter Sports

You get it. I'm pretty sure we could come up with more, and even sub-subcategories—like, aren't there a whole bunch of kinds of archery? Bookstores give you a chance to pick the setting and the main characters too. Let's say we're looking for an idea for our lead character. They're good at something. What? What is this person about? We wander about the aisles, flitting past sections in our mind (or in person), and we feel, we sense, we intuit creatively something in one section. Who knows what that will be? But what if it's, I don't know—it doesn't really matter, if we're just playing—but what if it's the self-help section? What if our character wants to be better so badly, they are reading every single self-help, inspirational book they can find?

This is just a starting point. We're writers; we'll layer in turning points along an arc. But for now, this is where we begin. Or we decide our protagonist is a self-help author, an expert in making people feel better, except that she has one problem. And we'll add that when we're ready, but for now, we've got two solid options to play around with and find our way with, just starting with something that interests us. We can easily do the same when Greek history catches our creative mind's eye. Who are the characters that fit in that world, are experts in that world, or even are fish out of water in that world? Who are we going to embody while we write? Who is it that lives in this world? Someone who belongs, someone who doesn't, someone who is ruling it, someone who is hating it, someone who is trying to escape it?

I encourage you to play this game on a regular basis to build up the speed with which an idea for a story can come to you. Get it *lit* up! Ahh! As you can see—with this game, ideas will always be plentiful. Why? Because you're an idea machine!

- Head to your favorite bookstore.
- Go to three sections that interest you.
- Pull out a couple of books from each that intrigue you.
- Narrow down your selections to a couple of books that, when you look through them, you can feel your imagination kick-starting itself.
- Purchase one or both of them.
- Choose a subject to write about. (For this one I'm choosing to write about doll furniture.)
- Choose a location that would or does exist in this world. (The attic of a huge doll mansion.) (My copyeditor suggests you read the Robert Aickman novella *The Inner Room*. Avoid spoilers!)
- Now, create a character that is from whatever world you've been looking into with these books. Just get an idea of someone who might be in this place, this setting you've described. (I am selecting a doll with a missing arm.)
- Set your timer for five minutes.
- Write about this someone you would find in this setting, describing them, their endowments, their way of looking at life, and so on. (I write about my doll; maybe I get into what happened to her arm, who took care of her, abandoned her, and so on.)
- Reset your timer for five minutes.

- Write, as that character, about what it's like to be them or about what is important to them. (I write, as the doll, how I'm looking forward to being discovered by the new family I hear moving in right now. There are children!)
- Again, when the timer goes off, you can always just keep going or reset the timer for a few minutes if you're on a roll.

Good job!

EXAMPLE

Let's say we pick science. Now, how does that help us come up with a cool setting or an interesting character? Well, we have to IMPRO-VISE a little. Hee hee! What are the places that come to mind when we start to think about places having to do with science? Did you think lab??? Did you? Okay, I did. I also thought basement. But now I have choices and will write a scene in one of those places or combine them and write about a caged creature in a lab in a basement. Creeeeeepy!

Even that one answer that several of us may have come up with is a gateway to many others. How many kinds of labs can there be? Dexter's lab, evil mastermind lab, lab with rats in charge and humans as the test subjects, drug testing lab, mascara developing lab, Einstein's lab, an Egyptian mummy's lab! (See, we can cross-pollinate with history or other sections of the bookstore. There are no rules!)

If we want to find a character, who are some of the people we think of who exist in this world? Who are experts in this world? Scientists, of course, but our leads can also be lab rats, orangutans, doctors, lobbyists, technicians, and so on.

QUICK TIP: Idea Flow

Be willing to let go of some of your ideas. Only time and reader/
audience response can tell you if your idea is a fantastic one or one
that just hasn't caught on. So don't try to shoehorn something into your
story just because *you* think it's the bee's knees. Try instead to stay in
the moment as you're writing and let the characters and momentum
and flow take you where they may. You can always see in editing if it
still needs your "great" idea or talk it over with your editor, but if it's not
part of the vibe, it might be best to save it for somewhere else.

Settings

Settings are sometimes so good, so well developed, they become a character in a story. Like Paris, in basically every movie set there, the Shire in the *Lord of the Rings* trilogy, the Bat Cave in *Batman*; you get the idea. They engage us, consume us, inspire us.

Where a story is set is integral to the telling of that story. And if you're like me, you set every one of your romantic comedies in a pastry shop with the female lead as the pastry chef and then realize at some point you've already written that story. It's the same thing onstage. I have my go-tos. But I also *love* getting knee deep in a scene in a new world that in real life I know nothing about, but because I have agreed to commit, to be an expert, I go to a new level of my own creativity and knowledge base. Pushing the envelope, as it were.

We're going to do an exercise that, when done onstage, creates a strong visual for an audience and everyone on a stage where, in reality, nothing exists. When our place in which the story is happening is fully formed—and we immerse ourselves completely in it, with commitment—the world and the characters are enriched.

#theresnoplacelikehome

GAME: Paint the Scenery

I invite you to be more descriptive than you normally might be, spend a little more time on setting than in the past, and get as specific as you possibly can (remember Five Objects—All Very Specific?).

▼ WHY ON EARTH WOULD WE DO THIS?

You can use this improv exercise to create lush landscapes, barren deserts, and everything in between to develop settings that could be drawn, painted, molded, sculpted, inhabited. It will be glorious. It will inspire stories, and then help keep you motivated to move through the story to completion. And just as it happens onstage, when we are given a location to begin with, characters just start showing up. There they are. And they're often pretty interesting.

- Set a timer for ten minutes.
- Choose a number from 1 through 50.
- Find your number in the Settings list, page 201. (Feel free to also use your memory or imagination, or visit your favorite library or bookstore and choose a location that way—then you're not becoming reliant on this book. Can you come up with one specific location? Not just Germany, but where exactly in Germany? Right? A zoo or a club or a certain character's kitchen or . . .)
- Go there with your wild imagination, you!
- Describe, flow, even if you haven't been there. Let yourself go and create an environment in the place you have chosen.

Ta-da!

EXAMPLE

A lone car sits at the side of the highway, smoke rising from its black shell. It is a husk of something that once shuttled life. An old Prius. Tinted windows, but not so dark as to hide that there is nothing inside but an empty Milk Duds package. Dots of chocolate stick to the console. A plastic water bottle rolls awkwardly across the highway, misshapen from the heat. Empty also.

Two sets of footprints head into the desert and begin to disappear in the distance.

Beyond them, in the same direction, is a craggy rock formation. A shrub or two. No shade to be found for hours. A piece of red fabric dangles from the shrub. A torn jacket? A message? Where did this couple go? Are they still alive?

In the other direction, a semi approaches noisily. Up until then, the only sound was the bottle hitting against the melting rubber tires.

A lizard circles a small rock on the side of the road, climbs atop it, conquering it. At least something is alive here. . . .

BONUS EXAMPLE

I also did this from a certain character's viewpoint. I recently got back from spending some time watching gorillas and monkeys and tigers. So I chose jungle. As you can see in both of these, characters started to show up. It's okay if they do or don't. No restrictions here. Like all the games and exercises here, they are yours to play with. Improv is for the people!

My foot crunches something underneath it. I look down. A rattlesnake skin. On the path? I wonder about this snake. One so busy it has shed its skin in the middle of a well-traveled trail. Or perhaps some other animal was dragging it? For what? Is that a thing? Could another animal use this one's excess for a nest? Certain birds do that. I've seen similar things in Central Park.

A twig snaps. I look up. High above, in the canopy, a family of monkeys swing back and forth. I wonder if they're the safest animals here. Moving so fast, so easily from one area to another. And here I am, standing look at a cast-off snake skin, about to be eaten. My own stomach gurgles in disagreement. Hunger is moving in. It's been three days since my own last meal. If you don't count the snails from this morning. In Paris, they would have charged a fortune for that, but here, it's life in the jungle. . . .

Characters

Characters are the absolute bedrock of stories. Characters alone are the meat and potatoes of our story dinner. Two different analogies? Exactly. They are everything. We'll go along with odd artistic decisions if we are in love with the characters. In Character Land all is found. Intriguing people are all around us, and this chapter is an invitation to discover them and explore their emotions, goals, and physicality.

The more we, as writers, learn and dive into the deep pool of character, the more impact we have. The more power. Power! Mwah ha ha!

These games are here to help you develop characters, give them more depth, differentiate them, heighten them, and so on. This chapter is going to be a lot longer than any other in the book, and rightly so; you know, character is key! So we're going to play a lot of games that let us continue to learn about our characters, mix up the way we come up with or discover and deal with them, and also let us dig into how a character can or should change because of a situation, character, or circumstances. You can also decide that the character doesn't change or doesn't change that much, as in a series. Again, we're all about making specific choices that put you ahead of the game and can help you avoid generalization and stereotyping pitfalls. Some things you come up with are just a part of the game; others will make their way into projects you care about deeply. I've seen it happen over and over. There's so much goodness to mine here. Let's get going!

Here's a fun one.

A wildly successful show was started at one of the schools I studied; it grabs someone's social media account and does an entire show around what they find. This is similar to a classic improv game where you bring an audience member up on stage, get them to tell you a little about themselves, how their day is going, maybe where they work, and then the performers act it out—it's hilarious and so insightful. Guess what? You can do the same thing—well, similar—sitting right where you are.

GAME: Social Media Mania

This exercise can go much deeper than the surface silliness. You might even end up connecting with this stranger. Everyone has a story; see if you can begin to comprehend enough about this person from their profile(s) to get inspired to create a new kind of character, different from your usual cast.

It's a simple entry point that can be a tool if you desire to go far under the surface, to navigate the depths of a world that we, before we clicked on that profile, were unaware of.

WHY ON EARTH WOULD WE DO THIS?

Characters are literally everywhere! Argh! It's like an invasion—but for writers and performers whose jobs are to create them, it's a very good invasion of humanity—the oddballs, the weirdos, those trying to be normal, those failing, those succeeding, those bigger than life, those mousy ones, those troubled, those free. Social media offers an opportunity to observe someone we don't know well or at all. What someone publishes to the world or their friends can actually tell us a lot about them. Combined with photos and videos, we can get a very clear picture of a very real person and find inspiration from them. I am not suggesting that you make fun of people who really put themselves out there; rather, that you gather information for the great well and, again, to mix things up. Pick somebody different from you. Don't judge them; allow yourself to come to an understanding about them from what you can learn about their online presence, their internet footprint.

In this exercise, I'm asking you to dive into a pool of people you don't know and to observe, gather, be ignited by them. Maybe one day you'll work your way up to walking up to strangers on the street. But until then, try a little research from the comfort of your computer station.

- Select a social networking site. (Now, you can also come back and repeat this exercise with a specific project you have in mind—go to a site that would have people like that. For example, I'm working on a character who loves knit-bombing. Well, where are those people? Give you one guess. Many opportunities to be inspired by the pins on Pinterest. There are a lot of crafters on there!)

- Search around for a new profile—someone you don't know.

- Get a sense of who they are from what they put out there.

- Choose a number from 1 through 100.

- Find your number in the Objects list, page 195.

- Set the timer for five minutes.

- Begin writing as this person about this object (they just bought, stole, or acquired today). You can write a post or blog entry as them about their day and this object. There's an important reason they are sharing it; be sure to include that in their post. Extreme excitement about this object!

Note: If the object you choose doesn't match at first, try the exercise anyway. This is how improv works: magic happens! You can also do the exercise if you see a post of an object on their profile—maybe they are looking lovingly at an afghan, maybe you are inspired to write about why. Go for it. These games are yours to share, to adjust. You may find you get inspired by them to create a whole story by asking, "What if they . . . ?"

Good on you, mate!

GAME: Aunt Bertha

We're going to continue finding characters simply everywhere! Let's mine that fantastic force in your life known as your family. Some of our favorite over-the-top *Saturday Night Live* characters as well as characters in TV, film, and books have been based on family members of the writer. Don't worry; you can change as much as you need to, to keep Aunt Bertha from recognizing her wily self in your work later; for now, commit to channeling her.

WHY ON EARTH WOULD WE DO THIS?

You can do this as many times as you like to develop characters for your stories, allowing them to answer increasingly appropriate questions. It's a way to find insight into any character. Just change the questions to suit your needs.

- Select someone in your family, or very very close to you, if you've thought of someone larger than life who inspires you.
- Set the timer for five minutes.
- Become them.
- Write as them answering the question: "What do you believe in?" They can be giving a speech, their last words on this Earth, a pep talk; whatever comes to mind as their reason for sharing this (perhaps they aren't, and it's a journal entry they plan to burn), go with it!

Woo hoo!

GAME: Letter to Mother

Now, let's move on to those people we love to hate: villains. Give your protagonist a good challenge by creating a complex character that we might even have some empathy for.

WHY ON EARTH WOULD WE DO THIS?

Any of these character exercises are also meant for your antagonist. Sometimes villains in a story can come off as mustache-twirling, one-dimensional evil-doers. And if you've ever known someone who committed a crime, you know there's more to the story. You would see them as much more than the hand reaching out to steal, the gun-wielder. To act and become your villain will give you more understanding and empathy for them and will make the material, like life sometimes, complex.

- Set the timer for five minutes.
- Choose a number from 1 through 50.
- Find your number in the Antagonists list, page 187 (or use your own if you're working on a project).
- Write for five minutes, from this antagonist's point of view (first person), a letter to their mother.

Good job!

QUICK TIP: Create Change

Be sure to create change for your characters. We want our characters to change in improv, in scenes; it keeps them interesting. Change, of course is critical for characters in stories; we must have an arc, unless we are making a statement about a character's *not* changing.

GAME: Flawed

Just like all of us in real life, every character has a flaw; sometimes more than just one. In a well-told story, that flaw can be what brings about the demise or destruction or even the death of the character. It is the thing that, although problematic throughout the story, the character finds a way to overcome by the end, growing and changing in the process. Stories are often about change. The flaw a character has in the beginning, and the change that occurs because of their efforts to get past this issue keep us spellbound. Will she or won't she?

It can even be a trait that sounds innocuous, but when taken to extremes causes trouble, trouble, trouble. Or it can be the worst of the worst and is eventually overcome. Here we play with creating, discovering these very human traits.

We're going to write a letter—one that might lead you to a story, like many of these games. It is about a character who has—you guessed it—a flaw. Not just any flaw, but one that at some point in this game is going to be destroyed by their actions that come about as a direct result of that flaw.

WHY ON EARTH WOULD WE DO THIS?

Flaws are an important aspect of storytelling and, yes, humanity. We wouldn't be very true to life if we left these out. Sometimes we try to create these heroes to be, well, superheroes, but even when we do that, there must be something that can bring them down. Otherwise, we lose interest—I think simply because we know that we are all flawed in some way. No character, no person is perfect. Not really. Even though it feels good to hear. And I'll say it: You're perfect, you! What I mean is you're perfect as you are. And so are your characters, if they have a flaw. Kind of a mind-meta-trip there. But you get it.

Because you're perfect!

Remember: There are no mistakes in improv.

- Choose a number from 1 through 100.
- Find your number in the Protagonists list, page 198, and write it on the top of your page (or use one you've been working on).
- Give them a name if they don't have one yet.
- Choose another number from 1 through 50.
- Find your number in the Settings list, page 201, and write it underneath your protagonist.
- Choose a number from 1 through 50.
- Find your number in the Flaws list, page 189.
- Write that next to your protagonist's name.
- Set the timer for ten minutes.
- Write for five minutes as them, unaware or only mildly aware that they have this issue.
- Reset the timer for five minutes.
- Write as them, buckling under this flaw. What is going wrong in their life because of it?
- Reset the timer for five minutes.
- Write as them free from this flaw—they have moved past it or overcome it. It can be an apology letter, them stating their plans or regrets, or a Dear John–type letter.

Fabuloso!

QUICK TIP: Timing Is Everything

Remember, you can always adjust the timer to be shorter or longer, or go past it when you're on a roll! It's your time—heh, heh.

GAME: World's Worst

Now we're going to play a silly game. Another one? you say. Yes! And . . . it's terrible! It's the worst! We're going to take a person and make them really bad at their job or role in life. This is a reminder to be willing to create flaws in our characters, but a chance to be playful about it.

WHY ON EARTH WOULD WE DO THIS?

It's a fun game for coming up with ideas, and you must think of a million things from one central idea until you know it's time to move on. Yes, the lines are supposed to be funny, but who cares? Just shoot 'em out. No thinking! It's also just good practice at being mean and making characters do bad things. Which must become second nature to us to create real conflict.

- Set the timer for one minute.
- Choose a number from 1 through 50 (for an antagonist) or 1 through 100 (for a protagonist).
- Find your number in either the Antagonists or Protagonists list, page 187 or 198.
- Write as quickly as you can one for one minute, line after line of dialogue, the world's worst version of what that character would say.
- Reset the timer for another minute and do it again with a different character.

That was the worst! (So, really, the best!)

Good job!

World's Worst Thief

"Here, I took these candlesticks, but I thought maybe you would miss them, so I brought them back."

"Yes, officer, I was speeding. I also hit a few things back there. Pretty lumpy drive. Pretty sure the things with legs weren't potholes. Also, don't look in the trunk. I'm an innocent man here."

"No, this is *my* Corvette with your vanity plate on it—what a coincidence!

EXERCISE: Opposites

The things that define us—these traits or attributes, as many as we personally can come up with about ourselves—we can come up with for all our characters. They are as we are, susceptible and vulgar and beautiful and disarming and boisterous and plain and cantankerous. It's all there. We just have to look for it, imagine it, make it up. This is where the fun can really go full blast. What a riotous time, picking out elements as though shopping for a great recipe! Let's make a character who is unforgettable!

In this exercise, we're going to use those very specific things that you and I do. That Cousin Willy does. That the woman sitting across from you on the subway does. The challenging way that fella bellies up to the bar—the same challenging way he approaches everything. These things: imaginative, quirky, quiet, bad-to-the-bone, conservative— they are a filter placed over our human eyes. Knowing several of them for every single character who comes across our pages makes our people inhabiting the world we're creating very dynamic. And that's a good thing. Let's build something.

WHY ON EARTH WOULD WE DO THIS?

Life is a balance of good and evil, light and dark, yin and yang. Here is our little improvisational way of exploring that. It can also lead to some good comedy, because juxtaposition is a key component of that.

- Take one of your characters that you've worked diligently on developing.

- Create a list of their traits. Good and bad.

- Now, on a new page, create a new character by making a list of characteristics just the opposite of your original character's; for example:

  - Shy? Bold.

  - Indecisive and hesitant? Rash and impulsive.

  - Greedy? Generous.

- Set the timer for five minutes and let that newly created character rant on a subject from the Library Sections list, page 193, the Themes list, page 205, or a subject of your own choosing. Maybe something that this new character would hate, that your original character loves, is a devotee of, can't get enough of. Play!

- Now reset the timer, doubling the time.

- Write a scene with these two characters in a setting or premise. Choose one yourself or choose randomly from the Settings list, page 201, or the Premises list, page 196. I think you're getting the hang of how these games work, so please explore!

Excellent!

GAME: Emotional Roller Coaster

If we can really reach people, we can leave an impression; we can suggest change or tolerance or love or fun or flapjacks or simply a feeling that all is good. To connect like this, the most powerful, visceral way I know is through emotion. Allowing, giving, forcing, releasing the characters to an extent that we could not even tolerate, that we could only dream of; to deliver an array of sensation that sends the reader vertical, the viewer to the edge of the seat; that causes the laughs to rumble from deep within and the tears to begin at the edges of the eye and continue where they may—this is our work, all made possible by creating extraordinary characters in extraordinary situations.

When the writer has written well, the path to emotional response for your reader is journeyed with satisfying ease. What an exhilarating, exciting experience to feel the emotion from the writer—from a person hundreds of years ago, or in another country, another place!

We will be creating a scene using the lists in the appendix, selecting the characters and some different emotions, and writing out the scene to justify these random changes in tone, exploring how characters, like people in our lives, can change emotions on a dime and how that can affect and intensify a scene.

If you have ever had trouble exploring emotions for characters, you now have a new tool.

WHY ON EARTH WOULD WE DO THIS?

Like the Raise the Stakes game we'll play later, we are going to throw random circumstances at your character or characters to elicit a change in emotions; to discover, to deepen, to understand further. Now, you can also play this with a character you are working on; perhaps you want to explore how they would organically express a certain feeling (or suppress it, for some characters are good at hiding their emotions or are more stoic).

- Select two numbers from 1 through 40.
- Find your numbers in the Relationships list, page 201.
- Give them names and write a little about them—a short description of each.
- Select two numbers from 1 through 150.
- Find your numbers in the Emotions list, page 187.
- Write those emotions at the top of the page.
- Choose a number from 1 through 100 for your place.
- Find your number in the Settings list, page 201.
- Choose a number from 1 through 50.
- Find your number in the Premises list, page 196.
- Set the timer for three minutes.
- Start writing the scene with these two people in it, in this place, feeling the way they do.
- When the timer goes off, set it to go off again every minute, or keep resetting it.
- Each time the timer goes off, randomly grab an emotion. Don't purposefully select; choose a random number, or just point and choose, but don't get thinky about it. The whole idea is that the emotions are all over the place.
- Now let both characters have that one new emotion and continue writing the scene, justifying their reactions however you can. Maybe the emotion works, maybe you don't have to justify, but these characters feel this emotion strongly and continue the scene for a minute until a new emotion is thrown at them via your timer.

Awesome! I'm crying over here.

GAME: Emotional Scrambler

Now, if you really want to work on specific characters, here is the game for you! Let's really work your characters here, see how far they'll go, how much they'll hide or try to conceal. Remember to switch characters and let yourself feel these new emotions. If we were onstage, the audience would demand to *see* them or they wouldn't leave satisfied.

WHY ON EARTH WOULD WE DO THIS?

The purpose here is to put characters you already know through the wringer. See how they react in certain situations in a very organic way.

- Select a character you've been working on, a person whose emotions you want to explore.

- In advance, select a few emotions from the Emotions list, page 187. You're going to want to throw different ones at them— get a range of positive and negative assembled in a list.

- Select a setting for them from the Settings list, page 201— somewhere that puts them *out* of their element—and a premise to match from the Premises list, page 196.

- Set the timer to go off every minute.

- Start off with one emotion, writing in either first or third person, and every time the timer goes off, throw a new emotion at the character or into the situation.

- What emotion does that create for your character? Justify it in your writing as an improvisor would justify it onstage.

- Try again, adding another character who exists in the world of the character you've been working on. Put them through the emotional scrambler as well (each time the timer goes off, they both take on this new emotion and continue the scene in that emotion). To me, this step, with two characters, is where the game gets fun!

Great!

GAME: Gibberish

Gibberish is pretty much what it sounds like. You just begin talking without using actual words. It's quite freeing and fun. It lets thoughts and emotions and ideas come to you in this weird free-flowing way that is hard to explain, but simply different from how we speak and organize exactly what we want to say. It helps you let go of the patterns behind how we say what we're thinking. And it is clear that people can understand so much more from body language and tone than from words alone. It's not the words, it's the way we say them. And this is always a fantastic place to play when we writers get so caught up in the preciseness of each word. I'm not saying words don't matter; rather, that there's a great deal to gain from being the character and communicating without them.

Choose to play with someone or alone.

WHY ON EARTH WOULD WE DO THIS?

Because it takes the pressure off words. Which, I mean, come on, admit it, sometimes we can get a leeeeetle precious with words. Get ready to let go of inhibitions. (I hope you've been doing that!) You may need to shed any remaining self-consciousness to get anything out of this . . . I invite you, again, to let go of inhibition.

- Set the timer for three minutes.
- Choose a number from 1 through 50 (for an antagonist) or 1 through 100 (for a protagonist).
- Find your number in either the Antagonists or Protagonists list, page 187 or 198.
- If you're playing with a partner, have them choose a number from 1 through 90. If you're playing alone, choose one yourself.
- Find your number in the Library Sections list, page 193, using it as a starting point, either sticking to it or meandering away from it. Remember, there are no mistakes in improv!
- Begin speaking in gibberish until the timer goes off. A monologue. Be sure to change up your emotions and use your body;

get up, move around, let the character express freely. (You can have the list of emotions in the back of the book open, and if you are only changing from happy to sad, mix in lots of others.)

- If you're working with a partner, have them write down what they think is being said. When "translating," they should do their best to write freely and at the same time hear the changes of intonation and feeling. If alone, finish your monologue, then reset the timer for five minutes and write down a translation of what you were saying during your gibberish monologue.

- Play again. For partners, switch roles of talker and translator.

Good work, team!

GAME: Goals

Just as having an intention is important for getting work done, it is the lifeblood of characters, and goals are paramount for good storytelling. By playing a couple of games, writers can discover goals and new possibilities of direction or even simply hobbies for their characters that move the story forward and express the dimensions, complexities, and dualities of humanity in a truthful way.

WHY ON EARTH WOULD WE DO THIS?

The following games are all opportunities to get creative, to not think, to explore and discover. They are each a new way into learning more about, creating backstory for, and just *being* a character you care about. This may just lead to an interesting augmented reality part of your project. Many existing popular characters do this—they establish online a section of that character's life. The satirical rom-com drama *Jane the Virgin* did this with a social media profile that fans could interact with. I'm just saying people get paid to come up with creative profiles of popular characters, and here you are, doing it from the start.

Of course, you can also do this with a character you've already established or by forming your own human from the back of the book. This work can become an important aspect of the creation of your characters. There's no telling what will light you up with an idea that makes you feel like you are on fire! But you're certainly making room for it with these games. You might even discover an important goal you were looking for in this first one.

- Choose a number from 1 through 100.
- Find your number in the Protagonists list, page 198.
- Set your timer for five minutes.
- Write, as the character, the three most important tasks to accomplish today.
- What is the character's one goal to focus on for the year's quarter?
- In five years, where does the character want to be? In ten?
- Write, as the character, these goals until the timer goes off.

Good job!

GAME: Bucket List

Here's another angle to get into their world with: let's discover the most important things your character wants.

WHY ON EARTH WOULD WE DO THIS?

To further define your character's desires, any and all practice is good on this very important point of storytelling. When we really know what a character is after, especially the big picture, we create in readers a desire for the character, even if it's an empathetic villain, to get it.

- Choose a number from 1 through 50 (for an antagonist) or 1 through 100 (for a protagonist).

- Find your number in either the Antagonists or Protagonists list, page 187 or 198.
- Set your timer for five minutes.
- Until the timer goes off, write, as the character, the things this person would love, need, enjoy doing before dying. Make a bullet point list.
- When you're done, look over the list. What are the top three?

Way to work!

GAME: New Year's Resolution

Here's a fun one to find out from your characters themselves what they want to change about themselves. Are they feeling pudgy after all that holiday fudgy?

Let's excavate some juicy inner and more immediate goals. Remember to be as specific as this character might be, or as laissez-faire . . . it's *the character's* impending year.

WHY ON EARTH WOULD WE DO THIS?

To further define your character's desires, get a little more into their mind, and see how they think in a stream of consciousness style.

- Choose a number from 1 through 50.
- Find your number in the Protagonists list, page 198.
- Set the timer for five minutes.
- Write for five minutes about how *this* year is going to be and what changes you (your character) want to make this coming year.
- Include all the little side thoughts to look at later. There's insight there.

Nicely played!

The character I'm working on is a Type A high-powered executive protagonist.

Get Bob to give me that raise. He knows I deserve it more than Jerry.

Start going to yoga more.

Do a freaking headstand—for crying out loud, how many years have I been going to that ridiculously overpriced boutique studio and I still can't do one? It's costing me a fortune, and for what?

Consider canceling yoga studio membership by February if those teachers don't motivate me.

Get on the board for Puggy Pet Rescue. Bob goes there a lot, and he'll see how committed I am to taking his advice to be more rounded. Whatever that means.

Start meditating. See above.

Beef up my LinkedIn profile in case Bob makes a dangerous mistake by passing me over.

In fact, maybe take a few personal items out of the office, in case our meeting doesn't go well.

Set an intention for the meeting to go well. Tim Ferriss said something about setting intentions, I think.

Read Tim Ferriss's *The 4-Hour Work Week* again. Just to brush up.

GAME: New Choice

Now we're going to play with coming up with new ideas very quickly. Again, don't think, just write the first thing that comes to mind. Work rapid-fire to create an alternative word or phrase whenever the timer goes off.

WHY ON EARTH WOULD WE DO THIS?

We want to continue to release that voice in our head that judges everything we come up with. Working quickly, no planning, writing off the cuff helps with that. By forcing a character to make new choices in a split second at random intervals, the writer discovers more about the character and has more options.

- Pick two numbers for two characters from 1 through 100.
- Find your numbers in the Protagonist list, page 198. (Or use a character of your own.) We'll put them in a scene together.
- Choose a number from 1 through 50.
- Find your number in the Premises list, page 196 (or use your own premise).
- Set the timer to go off every thirty seconds or reset each time for thirty seconds.
- Begin writing the scene, keeping it active; they are doing something the entire time, but you're focused on writing the dialogue.
- Every time the timer goes off, you write a new choice in the current line of dialogue. Something that replaces the very word or phrase you were on when the timer goes off.
- Repeat, resetting the timer (getting a new choice) at least three or four times.

Good job!

I'm using my own character, Marge. She bakes a lot, so I'm putting her in a high-end competition in Paris. This is her, talking to her assistant about her plans to win. Her action is icing elaborate cupcakes at the same time.

> MARGE: I'm going to have to bring out the big cupcakes this time. No one in France will be able to stop themselves. The icing alone is—[timer goes off.]

New Choice!

> The cupcake skirts themselves will delight all.
>
> The lettering is going to blow some minds.
>
> The acou-tray-mon (French accent) is face-melting! [Timer goes off.]

New Choice!

> So, I feel like I pretty much have this whole competition in the bag. I mean, I understand I'm just a housewife from the Midwest, but I will represent!!! [Timer goes off.]

New Choice!

> I will dominate.
>
> I will make them eat cake!
>
> I will find a way into their little coeurs.
>
> I will weasel my way into my dream kitchen and bake in heavenly ways until someone screams arrêt!!!
>
> I will have my way with that chef!
>
> I will maybe put a little extra rum in all the cakes, not to cheat, but you know, to persuade. [The timer went off at some point . . . I was too busy competing as Marge to notice.]

As I wrote this, as a side effect, Marge's plans became even more clear, and I had some fun options to pick from to punch up the script afterward (make it a little more fun and funny; a little more *her*).

GAME: Hidden Agenda

Now we're going to write a scene in which one character has a hidden agenda. When I studied with my first improv teacher Gary Austin (who founded the improvisation and sketch comedy theatre the Groundlings), this was the first improv game I ever played. I still remember the secret I had against my "sister"—that's how powerfully these things can stay with us. It also taught me that when you're in the midst of creating it, a scene can go in many different directions, and that improv was not just for creating laughs. Although some hilarious scenes can come about with this game, too. . . .

WHY ON EARTH WOULD WE DO THIS?

This adds a dynamic element and a level of complexity to the scene. In giving your characters a hidden agenda, subtle nuances and motivations can emerge. If we're being truthful, most of us walk around every day with them.

- Pick two numbers from 1 through 100.
- Find your numbers in the Protagonist list, page 198.
- Choose a number from 1 through 40.
- Find your number in the Relationships list, page 201.
- Write it at the top of the page and give them names—even a little more description.
- Choose a number from 1 through 50.
- Find your number in the Premises list, page 196.
- Give one character in the scene a hidden agenda (the other character doesn't know about it) that the first character works throughout to achieve. Make it a goal that grows from the premise.
- Set the timer for five minutes.
- This can be simple or more involved. Get the other one to get them something to drink, get the other one to offer them the keys to the car, get them to leave you alone with their computer—you get the idea.

- Write the scene.
- If they are really in the thick of it, keep going.

Goodness, look at ya!

EXAMPLE

I chose boss and employee (Sandrine and Edward) who, while stranded on a deserted island for months, finally see a boat in the distance.

I give the boss the hidden agenda that she has been embezzling funds; she is pretty sure that the employee, Edward, knows about it, and she has decided to send him off on a food-gathering trip to get rid of him—promising he'll get back in time, knowing he won't.

I give the employee, Edward, the hidden agenda that he is going to write a book about how good his boss has been to him when they get off this island. Sandrine is the only one who ever believed in him.

I write the bittersweetness of this duo.

QUICK TIP: Keep It Active

Find ways to incorporate action into each scene so we have fewer talking heads—scenes with people just sitting around—and instead, more doing, more happening.

WARM-UP: Walkabout

The physical aspects of a character affect them as much as our own affect us. Selecting one or several can continue to help "flesh out" our players. See what I did there? I offer a list of these in the appendix to draw from, but they are everywhere: shapes and sizes and health factors, oh my.

In a script, when this is not provided, few actors add it. Most people don't think to add a hump without reason. Several of Shakespeare's characters are played with the same look for hundreds of years, because he wrote them that way with Richard III's hump or Falstaff's belly. Consider Edmond Rostand and his nose for the eponymous character in *Cyrano de Bergerac*. Whatever it may be, these physical choices can make your creations unforgettable.

You may find that these choices really affect the story and therefore the audience. They may be random now, but you know how to make meaningful choices. Again, we're exploring.

As this game suggests, we are going on a walkabout. And we are going to do it with the same level of commitment as a trained actor onstage, doing our best to stay in character the whole time, challenging ourselves to go outside our comfort zone. We did a short version of this with Character Shoes on page 60. This time we are creating a more complicated character, the way you would get to do in theater school once you start playing more complex parts. If you have never tried out an accent, do it now. Try out being someone very different from yourself. (But hey—if you create a kleptomaniac, I just want to say, here and now, you can't claim you stole that doughnut for a writing exercise. Play! But stay out of jail.)

WHY ON EARTH WOULD WE DO THIS?

This is for you—for character discovery. Feel free to layer several from the list in the back or, as always, make up your own, and discover how these changes inform a character's view and influence everything from their emotions to their actions. With the new cane she needs, that former athlete is no longer so willing to cross when the WALK light is flashing.

Since you're getting so good at all this, let's up the ante with a choice that can really change your physicality and, as you may have noticed in the last game, some of your thoughts too. As an example, if your character is constantly in pain, their thoughts are certainly reflective of their limited condition—just as it is in life!

- Choose a number from 1 through 50.
- Find your number in the Endowments list, page 189.
- Choose a number from 1 through 50 (for an antagonist) or 1 through 100 (for a protagonist).
- Find your number in either the Antagonists or Protagonists list, page 187 or 198 (or choose a character of your own).
- Set the timer for three minutes.
- Write about either how this trait affects them or how it developed. (They were born with it, car crash, or something else.)
- Now that you have this knowledge, commit to becoming them with this impediment (or advantage).
- Head outdoors for a short walk. Explore the world as this person, moving however they do. There is no right or wrong way to do this.
- Let go of any concern that anyone is judging you—no one even needs to know what you're up to.

Good job!

EXERCISE: Animal Essence

Now I am going to ask you to do something that may seem ridiculous, but it will test your willingness to apply some of these ideas and rules. I am going to ask you to get out of your head, to let go of judgment, and try something you may never have done before.

I am going to ask you to choose an animal from the Animals list or make up your own Animal Essence. It doesn't have to be about barking or full out becoming an animal (although it can). It's mostly about exploring the qualities of an animal in some way and allowing it to influence your understanding, creation, depiction of a character. Actors often look to nature, animals specifically, for inspiration.

WHY ON EARTH WOULD WE DO THIS?

Actors often study animals and their traits and, unwittingly or not, meld them into their creations. We can do the same.

It's not so much about crawling around your office on all fours—though I won't stop you. I've done it myself. I'm probably busy doing that right now. But seriously, folks, it's more about moving sensuously as a feline might, taking care to groom or caress herself, and so on. Not so much about lumbering awkwardly across the living room (I really won't stop you), but committing and moving in a graceful, predatory way—you dig?

Then try another animal, one close to your antagonist; same drill. But it's a totally different way of looking at the world and being in the world, maybe being more of a predator, maybe less.

Helpful tip: *Be* the monkey; don't think, because a monkey doesn't think tooooo much. The monkey just finds a clever way to get the grapes.

- Choose a number from 1 through 50.
- Find your number in the Animals list, page 186.
- Set the timer and spend about ten minutes reading about this animal. Watch a video of one if you can.

- Then set the timer again for two minutes. Using everything you have just learned about this animal, simply decide to become it.

- Allow yourself to move with the essence of this animal, make noises influenced by those your animal would make, do things keeping in mind how your animal does them—sipping (or slurping) coffee, watching the neighbors, opening a package, and so on.

- Don't stop until the timer goes off. Even if you feel ridiculous, well, that's okay. Commit and keep going to discover a new layer of possibility, a new way of looking at the world.

- Select a character you enjoy working on, or use the Antagonists or Protagonist lists on pages 187 and 198.

- Consider the different animals from the list of animals.

- Select one with attributes similar to some that your character seems to have.

- Set the timer for two minutes.

- Be very specific in taking on some of the key attributes of this animal—as your character. Posture, movement, speed, and the like.

- Become your character with some of these elements in mind. Allow yourself to explore movement in your space.

- Stay committed to this version of your character—you may even find your thoughts become more predatory or fearful.

- When the timer goes off, return to us, please!

Good stuff!

GAME: Rashomon (Point of View)

All characters have relationships, and a full exploration of them can yield a very rich manuscript. It is one of the most important aspects of humanity—how we relate to one another. And it's one reason improvisation is often taken into businesses and classes and groups: to teach team building, working with one another, getting on the same page. We can do the exact same thing through improv with our characters.

I *love* this improv game, maybe because I enjoy looking at issues from all angles—but come on! This is intricate storytelling. Have fun with this one!

This game is based on Akira Kurosawa's great film *Rashomon*, which features the telling of a story through the different viewpoints of several characters. We will establish a scene, making very sure it's clear how the four characters relate to each other. Then we will tell the same story again, from each of the four people's points of view—how they saw the same scene and what they were thinking, feeling, doing will come forward. Oh, get ready for a ride!

WHY ON EARTH WOULD WE DO THIS?

This is a powerful way to discover more about all the characters in your work and to give each part care and time as well as to connect how these characters really feel about each other and interrelate. This is a deep dive into the thoughts of every character in your story and can be done beyond just playing the game to loosen up and have fun. You can take a scene from a story that you are working on, even struggling with, apply this style, and voilà! You have your mojo! Because now you have firsthand experience acting and writing as each character right there in your seat, and thoughts may flood you, but hey, isn't that better than chewing on your No. 2 all day long?

It is an information-gathering mission, but keep in mind, the time invested in this form can yield a finished piece if crafted with your own personal explosive artistry and style. I encourage you to go further and use this game on every character in your story; play with emotions, premises, and so on. Rah!!!

- Choose a number from 1 through 100.
- Find your number in the Protagonists list, page 198 (or use your own).
- Choose two numbers from 1 through 50.
- Find your numbers in the Antagonists and Supporting Players lists on pages 187 and 204 (or use your own).
- Set a timer for three minutes.
- Decide on a certain kind of experience (exhilarating, intense, whatever) your protagonist has just been in that involved your selected antagonist character and your supporting player. If you aren't coming up with one from what you know or imagine about the character, choose something from the Premises list, page 196.
- Write, as your protagonist, about this experience.
- Reset the timer for the same amount of time.
- Write the same scene from the second character's point of view, keeping in mind they will likely have vastly different thoughts on this experience as well as emotions.
- Reset the timer for the same amount of time.
- Write the same scene from the third character's point of view— again, through their eyes.
- Review this piece and marvel at all the new information that was just sitting there!

Great job!

EXAMPLE

I chose a bossy little girl (age eight) crying on a swing in a park next to a hospital, a nurse watching her, and a dog nearby, crouching closer—a tableau I actually saw once and wanted to write a version of.

GIRL

All I wanted was to come outside, and no one would let me. No one listens to me. They just poke at me and expect me to keep smiling and forget that I'm a lab rat. Well, I'm not. I'm not a lab rat. I think lab rats might even have it better than me. This funny dog, who probably doesn't even have a home, looks happy to be out here. Uh, and she won't leave him alone either. And Mean Nurse won't stop bossing me around. Why does she even work at this stupid hospital? Aren't nurses supposed to be nice? All the nurses are nice. They were until she showed up. They let me do what I want. If I want ice cream, they bring it. If I want to go outside and feel the sun, they let me. Not her. No, I never asked to come to the park before, but still, they'd let me. And why did they even put a stupid park next to a stupid hospital if they don't let anyone use it? Why? I just want to be left alone. Just staring at me. Mean nurse. Kah. Here doggy! Maybe he understands. Oh! Ah, he's so cute!

NURSE

If I don't get Abigail inside in the next two minutes, three things are going to happen independently. One: I'm going to lose my job. Two: She's going to get worse than she already is and further expose her already weak immune system. Three: This mangy dog is going to give one of us rabies. Why did I ever take this position? I knew I would never be cut out to work with sick kids. I was a sick kid. I hate watching her get worse every day. Those other nurses let her do whatever she wants, but she needs some discipline. And somehow I feel like I need to see her every day. She's been here longer than me, and one day I'm going to come in and she's not going to be here and all I can think is that I should have dragged her back inside. Just like I should drag this dog to the pound. But I can't even seem to get my feet to move. How can you drag a crying, dying child from a swing back inside. I can't. I can't, and I'm going to get fired and this is the first job I was ever good at. A job I don't even like. Oh no! It's on the move! It's . . . it's. . . .

DOG

I wish I could lick her hand. There's salt on her hand. The tears need to go. Tears are very overrated. I mean, I've had use for them from time to time, but humans use them a lot. Maybe they feel better when they are done? I feel better when I have a snack. If I had a snack I would share it with the little one dangling her feet. If I was human I would go right up there and put my arm around her and tell her everything was going to be okay. I would let her know that right now things seem tough, but it's all okay. It's all temporary, we're temporary. I think she would get that, because the smaller humans are always more intelligent than the big humans. Like that other big human; she'd call canine cops in if she could. But I'm not going anywhere. Not until this little one smiles. Ooh—she's giving me the signal. Goin' in! I'm gonna get her to smile! Yes I am!

GAME: Dear Diary

Now here's another game to create in the exact way your character would.

We're going to write some entries delving into their innermost thoughts about the people closest to them. Get juicy! They believe no one will ever see this and are just letting it *all* out.

Use a computer if they are a Type A executive who would do so or a rainbow-colored locking journal if it's a character who records their deepest thoughts this way, or whatever fits. Get out there and carve on a rock face if they're prehistoric. You know the drill: have fun with this. You can even shop for a diary for your favorite gossipy character if you want to take it there. I encourage whatever makes this experience more playful and fun, whatever leads to further discovery and a possible aha! moment!

WHY ON EARTH WOULD WE DO THIS?

This lets you spend even more time as a character, allowing their ideas, desires, and dislikes bubble to the surface and be revealed to you. You know, this can be huge chunks of your book, or your entire book may even end up written this way. We have plenty of examples of successful stories told in this way. We won't write an entire novel right now, here, but you can. I urge you to.

What I really like about this game is that the pressure is off; you can get a lot of material sourced that can be a part of the final piece, or you can let it be simply information gathering. But for sure, you'll know your characters a lot better and discover a lot more, writing as them. Remember how low-pressure journaling is? It can be deep, pour-your-heart-out secrets or a bit of what was had for lunch—or a mix. Anything goes, and again, there's no wrong answer. The character tells and informs us of so much—we must just be the conduit and step into being them with full commitment, and our world will explode with detail and life and possibility.

- Select a character of your own or choose a number from 1 through 100.
- Pull your character from the Protagonist list, page 198.
- Set your timer for five minutes.
- Write as your character, starting with "Dear Diary" (or however else your character would write down their innermost thoughts).
- Repeat this until you have several entries.

Lovely!

EXAMPLE

I have a character who has a specific name for her diary, has given her (yes, the diary's female) traits, and talks to her like a best friend—she not only expresses in it how she really feels about her friends and family, but she has a relationship with her diary. This further defines the character, and I learn a lot about her each time. These tidbits may or may not make it into the finished project but are a whole lotta fun, y'all! (She's Southern as can be!)

Premises

**In working to come up with a succinct definition for "premise," I
found a wide range of definitions in the discussion among successful writers.**

In television animation, when a premise is turned in as a blueprint
for the episode, it usually reveals which characters will drive this story,
what problem or issue they are up against, and the ways they will attempt
to overcome it, leading to and inclusive of the resolution.

But I've also come across very simple definitions that could be
exchanged with the term "logline": a simple statement that sums up the
story and its essence.

There's also the work we do in constantly asking, "What if . . . ?" or
"What would happen if . . . ?"

Then there is how Robert McKee encapsulates it, which I think suits
our purpose and our games very well, because he says "a premise is rarely
a closed statement."

Aha! Go on, McKee:

"What would happen if . . ." is only one kind of premise. Writers
find inspiration wherever they turn—in a friend's lighthearted

confession of a dark desire, the jibe of a legless beggar, a nightmare or daydream, a newspaper fact, a child's fantasy . . . anything may premise the writing, even, for example, a glance out a window.

Well, there it is—an invitation to play our next game!

The point is to take all these games and lists and tools and run with them. Wildly.

#nicetomeetyou

GAME: Headlines

Headlines is a great game for coming up with premises. In improv, we don't spend too much time thinking (NONE! Ha ha!) before we begin creating, so this game gives that gift too. Your premise already exists. Have you noticed how your favorite procedural show is doing an entire episode on something that smells very similar to the dead body found in a NYC apartment building last month? Dark, but we New Yorkers know it's true. Many writers and producers have admitted to getting their ideas from scouring the headlines in the newspaper. Your turn.

So if you want maybe a heavier situation, check out the headlines. Sometimes you'll find some funny stuff too. The stuff of life! You've got your settings to play with, and, most importantly, you've got a character you understand. Now let's put them in a headline-making situation and see how they handle that. If the headlines are all too dark for your genre, lighten them up or make up your own headlines that fit. With Headlines, we are pulling double duty by getting an angle that covers current events. For artists, being relevant is key.

WHY ON EARTH WOULD WE DO THIS?

This is another testament that there are innumerable possibilities for stories out there. Every time I wade through stories looking for comedic material, I am rewarded with extensive fodder.

And sometimes the sweetest story can be a jumping-off point for a story you never expected to find yourself writing. This is a great way to shake up your writing and even choose another genre to tell a story in. Like all the other games, this one brings continued self-discovery for a writer. What stories are you drawn to? Be sure to look on sites that aren't all doom and gloom either. I mix it up, going to different sites that offer more unusual fare. Even clickbait can provide material.

We're not the first to cultivate work this way—but it will always be our job to write with authenticity when we choose the one or two stories that impact us out of the thousands and thousands out there daily.

In improv, we don't retell the story verbatim—no, we exaggerate and play and expand and push. I invite you to get flexy with it!

- Do a quick search on news for today.
- Look through the recent headlines, or scan the Headlines list, page 193.
- Select one as quickly as if someone from the audience were giving you a suggestion (but also something that piques your interest).
- Set the timer for five minutes.
- Use this headline as *inspiration* to write a retelling of it using a character you create from lists in the back (Protagonists, Antagonists, or Supporting Players on pages 198, 187, or 204, or one you've been working on).
- Write until the timer goes off.

Excellent!

You can't make this stuff up! Sometimes I wish I was.

Oh wait, I am. Hooray!

EXERCISE: Premises—Built to Order

As you will see, you have as many options as you want for your characters; you can tailor them for yourself, too, by writing a list of your own. Tailor from the Headlines list or Premises in the back of the book on pages 193 and 196. They can be as simple as these:

- **Getting arrested for the first time**
- **Witnessing a stranger jump in front of a train**
- **Getting proposed to or proposing marriage**

The point is for you to create your own list that inspires you. You can keep it handy as your own personal prompt list. I encourage you to do this, because I wrote the ones in this book, and I can get a little silly with my lists, and not everyone needs big, bold characters in bizarre situations. To start you off, I'm leaving a blank in the list in the back for you to add one for the genre that suits you best.

Give it a try! You are a fabulous writer, after all. Have fun, explore. Use all that creativity that's juicing you up. You can get real niche, too! For example, if you write fantasy, go ahead and write your own list, either made up off the top of your head or based on a project you have been developing. Maybe your character list looks like:

- **Wizard**
- **Gargoyle**
- **Fairy**
- **Troll**

Or with specific names from your script or novel:

- **Wizard of Eretheron**
- **Fancy Gargoyles of Pincer**
- **Chocolate Fairy (um, what's that? What did you just make up?)**
- **Mega-Troll**

Your premises might look like:

- **Our heroine learns of a power she didn't know she had**

- Escaping on the back of the Primordial Beast
- Coming out of a long sleep

Or in another genre—say you like to write romantic comedies, so maybe you have a whole list of situations for the meet-cute, you know, that sweet, surprising, funny, or interesting way the two lead characters (who are going to have some kind of romantic relationship) connect? The meet-cute can have a lot to do with the concept of the project:

- They meet at a therapy group for love addicts.
- They meet waiting in court as witnesses in the same case.

You can do these same steps with any genre you want to work in. Every genre has its own rules of that world. Tropes. These are studied in improvisation when games are played and stories told in different genres. We can do them too to come up with our next passion project or when we are hired to write in this other arena.

- Study your genre of choice, looking for the laws of this style until you're comfortable with your knowledge of it.
- Set the timer for five minutes.
- Create a list of settings for this genre.
- Reset the timer for five minutes.
- Create a list of protagonists that could exist in this world.
- Reset the timer for five minutes.
- Create a list of antagonists too.
- Reset the timer for five minutes.
- Create a list of premises for possible stories—you don't have to flesh these out (although you can if you get excited by one idea; that's the whole point).
- Put these lists up around you and play some of the games in this book with them or, if you're ready, start working with your story.

Great!

> For millions of years, mankind lived just like the animals. Then something happened which unleashed the power of our imagination. We learned to talk and we learned to listen. Speech has allowed the communication of ideas, enabling human beings to work together to build the impossible.
> —STEPHEN HAWKING

Dialogue

Dialogue is a combination of two words: *dia*, the prefix meaning two, and suffix *-logue*, tongue or speaking. We've done an improvised monologue in Making of a Monologue and Rashomon (Point of View), and now we move on to two people talking. You already know how to do this, but we're going to provide all the information you need to build a strong scene in a few seconds.

Scenes are the building blocks of a longer piece. If you can create a great scene once, moving an audience emotionally throughout it with changing characters, you can do it enough times to hold an audience spellbound through the entire arc of your story or book.

QUICK TIP: Stay out of CrazyTown

CrazyTown is a place in ImprovLand where improvisors can easily go. It happens when they add information that can't possibly be true or that denies or contradicts things that their partner set up. There's a good county line between unique, creative, and original and plain crazy. Stay out of that district. You lose the audience's trust.

GAME: Three Lines

Improv scenes have a beginning, middle, and an end, even if they are very short. If they are short, the clarity must be there. In improv, complete clarity in the first couple of lines is important—we need to know who these characters are to each other, where they are, and what they are doing—what this scene is about. And this little game does all of that in three lines.

WHY ON EARTH WOULD WE DO THIS?

To be concise. To practice getting the important information out immediately. Subtlety can actually be the kiss of death in improv. This gives your scene immunity. If we can do this now, and quickly, without thinking, it will become a natural thing that we can always do. Wouldn't it be neat to know you can come up with an entire premise, with no thinking, in a split second? You can! You just did!

- Set the timer for five minutes (remember, you can lengthen or shorten the time if you're a fast/slow writer or typist).

- We'll get any scene started and going with the
  - who
  - what
  - where

  in three lines!

- Character 1 gives a line that reveals what these two are doing: "It's so fun to go shopping with you." Or you might have some thought of some story one of them wants to tell.

- Character 2 gives a line that tells us where we are: "I love all the styles Victoria's Secret has in right now!"

- Character 1 also gives the relationship: "Well, Gramma, I really appreciate your making time for me."

- These can be in any order. Place first, or relationship and whatever the activity or action is. Sometimes you'll find you can land them all in two lines. I love working that way myself. In this exercise, let's just get the info out in the first two to three lines in a few seconds; not too much thinking needed here.

- Repeat this exercise a couple of times. We're going to find new characters we are excited to write about and then build a scene. If it was hard to get the who, what, where out in those three lines, keep practicing this game. It's a really good one to master, and if you ever end up onstage, it will save the day. Once you feel really good about your ability to provide all this info in a matter of a couple of minutes every time, move on to the next version.

Nicely played!

GAME: Three Lines—Unstoppable

In this extension of the previous exercise, you'll write a scene with a beginning, middle, and end. We'll get into that even more in Plot/Structure games, but for now, we are building on our skill, in the moment, to come up with something immediately, without thinking about it as we start to move into some form of story structure.

WHY ON EARTH WOULD WE DO THIS?

Scenes are the building blocks used to create the foundation of stories. Any time spent at this smaller, cellular level is time very well spent strengthening our story-making muscles. There are certain things we want to have happen in scenes. They propel us further along in the journey and are the places wherein key elements happen. They are also a place where we can see a character's inner turmoil butt up against an external goal.

So here is a chance to practice all that while continuing to build your dialogue muscle. Each character has a specific goal that they want, in the novel or play or film as a whole, but also in this particular scene. The other characters or circumstances get in the way, create obstacles and issues and just generally make life and the overall story much more interesting. So, basically, let's just lob a lot of problems at our lead character, either through things happening to everybody, or the other character(s) creating full-on roadblocks between your character and what your character wants.

- Now choose one of the three lines you just did that you liked the most.
- Set the timer for five minutes and continue with lines of dialogue.
- Build the scene from what you have—if you have not established a clear goal (I know these arbitrary lines get in the way, but they have their playful purpose), choose now. Your lead REALLY needs _____.
- Move forward, throwing issues, obstacles, and problems in their way every chance you get.
- Then let it come to a close naturally.
- If the timer goes off and you're not at the end, go ahead and write the ending. Get your character to a place different from where the scene started.

Woo hoo!

Character 1 gives a line that reveals what these two are doing: "It's so fun to go shopping with you."

Character 2 gives a line that tells us where we are: "I love all the styles Victoria's Secret has in right now!"

Character 1 also gives the relationship: "Well, Gramma, I really appreciate you making time for me."

So we know who they are, and we move into this dialogue:

Gramma: I figure I best keep you out of trouble. I really don't like that boy you're dating.

Granddaughter: Oh! Roger? Things have actually gotten quite serious. We started talking about—

Gramma: Don't you dare tell me you are thinking about getting married, Josie.

Josie: I think he might propose; that's actually why I wanted to come here, to pick out something nice–

Gramma: Nothing here will fit you. I asked; let's go.

Josie: But–

Gramma: Don't "but" me. This is the whole problem; you're too stubborn. I'm going to set you up with that nice Clarence from down the street.

Josie: He's 12!!

Gramma: He'll mature. And then you'll be old enough to know better than to marry anyone.

[Gramma drags her out by her arm.]

GAME: "I Just Have to Say"

Let's play a challenging game writing a scene with just dialogue. We're going to use an existing article, script, or book for the lines of dialogue. You may be challenged with trying to make the line make sense, but do your best to explain or justify it as naturally as you can.

WHY ON EARTH WOULD WE DO THIS?

This can get silly, but if you stick with your character, you might just learn a little more about them. Part of the point is to get to a place where dialogue is not precious. Let it flow. Let it go wherever it goes. You can always (and you will) come back later and edit. But for now, try writing a scene this same exact way with the three lines, different characters, and no timer, no random lines, just characters made up on the spot, talking.

- Find a play, magazine, or novel.
- Play Three Lines from the last section to get this started.
- Character 1 (unrelated to the play, magazine, or novel—the characters will start to tell us who they are, at least to each

other, by the third line) gives us a line that reveals what these two are doing: "Nice day for fishing."

- Character 2 gives us a line that tells us where we are: "I've never seen the lake this high before."

- Character 3 gives us the relationship: "Dad, I remember the first time you ever brought me out here."

- Again, these can be in any order. Let's just get the info out in the first two to three lines.

- Set the timer to go off every minute for the next ten minutes.

- Continue to write dialogue now that you know what they are doing. Go back and forth with this conversation, as these two would in life.

- Open up the play, book, or magazine to any page with print. As the one-minute timer goes off, let whatever character is speaking say (writing it for them) "I just have to say:" and look down at the open page.

- Whatever your eye falls on, say that as a line in character, as this character's own idea. You may find you don't always need the "I just have to say" line; in fact, the more you work your way toward natural ways of getting these totally random lines in, the better. In a live show, the audience loves the surprise, the randomness, and the commitment to both.

- As each person says something [ridiculous], they may have to justify, as realistically as possible, why this came out of their mouth. The justifying must come *after* they have said the line, not before, so there's no time to think of a reason for saying it, but just to say it to the other.

- Go back and forth with lines of dialogue for ten minutes or so—you may find, as with some of the other games, that you want to keep going.

Fantastic, my friend!

GAME: The Alphabet Game

Ooh, this next one is one of my favorites! (I feel like I say that for 110 percent of these!) Don't let yourself get stuck in your head; keep moving, keep writing, even if it's weird. We're just playing!

We're going to have a couple of characters in this scene talking, but their dialogue must be in alphabetical order. Yup. The first character to speak starts their sentence with a word that starts with "A." The other character responds (and hopefully makes some sense) with a line of dialogue that starts with a word beginning with "B." Each line that follows must start with a word that begins with the next letter in the alphabet.

WHY ON EARTH WOULD WE DO THIS?

By using the restriction of each character's line of dialogue beginning with the next letter of the alphabet, the writer is forced to focus on something other than free-flowing conversation. Everything is easier after this doozy!

This game, like many others, sidesteps writer's block. It keeps you from focusing on being blocked by putting your attention on other things.

- **Set a timer for seven minutes.**
- **Choose a number from 1 through 40.**
- **Find your number in the Relationships list, page 201. (You can also use your own or grab two characters from the Protagonist or Antagonist lists.)**
- **Choose a number from 1 through 50.**
- **Find your number in the Premises list, page 196.**
- **Focus solely on writing dialogue.**
- **Alternate between the characters; they get one line each, and the sentence they speak must begin with the next letter of the alphabet.**

- See if you can get through the entire alphabet, have a scene that somewhat makes sense, and have some fun.
- Write until the timer goes off.
- Try again and this time make it harder by choosing a different letter of the alphabet to start on. (Don't cheat and have the alphabet in front of you! Sneaky. I'm watching you!)

Write on!

Two Coworkers Trapped in Someone's Dungeon

Character 1: All right, I'm sorry I got us into this, but I think I know a way out.

Character 2: Back home! That's the only place I want to be right now.

Character 1: Course it is. You haven't stopped talking about it since they tossed our sorry sacks down that garbage chute.

Character 2: Don't you blame me.

Character 1: Excuse me! No one is blaming you. I did say I had an idea. . . .

Character 2: Fine. Out with it. It better be good, Rufus.

I randomly selected Productive Passport Officer and Focused Cheerleader from the Protagonists list, page 198. To save time, I didn't write out the names for each line. I hope that the character speaking will be clear. It's a sign of good dialogue that it is clearly characteristic of the person saying it.

Ahem, Miss, I need your passport.

But I told that guy I don't have it.

C'mon, you're old enough to know how this works.

Don't say things like that. That's what my dad says, and it drives me nuts.

Each time I have to spend this amount of my day explaining the rules to someone like you, that's time I don't get to go on my break and watch WWE.

Forget about wrestling! I'm having a real problem, and you know what?

Guh! What?

Holy! Help! I can feel it!

I can't help you if you don't tell me what's going on.

Just so you know–I'm about to have a complete and total melt-down.

Kicking and screaming? I've seen it before.

Look–

Miss–

No! I am not a miss!

Oh! Okay, excuse me. Ma'am.

Please quit picking on me and let me through the security thingy!

Quit. Picking. On. You?

GAME: One-Word Story (Writing Partner Time!)

The band Postal Service created hit songs by using the same concept that we are about to use in this game. The musicians, Ben Gibbard (also of Death Cab for Cutie fame) and Jimmy Tamborello, really wanted to work together but lived too far away from each other to rehearse and write together, so they started sending versions of their song back and forth through the U.S. mail. That is also how they came up with their name. Bizarrely funny note: The U.S. Postal Service sent the band a cease and desist letter because of their name, but ending up negotiating that the government would let them keep it if they helped with promotion. Isn't that nuts? I shouldn't be surprised, because the school that I graduated from, IO West, used to be called Improv Olympics. But guess what? The International Olympic Committee also told them to change the name—or else. But I digress. (Ah, so this is what that feels like!) Anyway, back to the band—Jimmy would create beats and mail them to Ben, who would edit and add to it his own melodies. He'd mail it back, and they'd go back and forth. Interestingly, no lyrics were added until everything else was there.

Kinda like building your story with an outline or plot and then going back and adding some dialogue? (Am I digressing again? You gotta watch out for me, I tell ya.)

So I'm happy to introduce this next gem to you, because it's a foundational type of game. It has all the basics, and you actually have a story at the end of it. You are free to play it at your next party; just be sure to explain a couple of basic improv rules, because without any of them—especially the all-important support of instant agreement—this party trick can tank faster than, you know, a tank edging off a short pier.

You're going to tell a story that has never been told before. You'll do it one. Word. At. A. Time. You say ONE word, your partner says the next, and you go back and forth until you have told a story and fulfilled the title. (If the story is the little black hen that cried tears of licorice drops, you better have—what? Yes, a black hen. Tears of licorice drops. And the earlier you can fulfill this, the better.) It's easy to forget that part, but like a good premise or logline, it can keep us in StoryLand and out of CrazyTown. Also, be sure to have a few lines of dialogue that add to the story said by each character who is mentioned.

WHY ON EARTH WOULD WE DO THIS?

This creates synchronicity in a writing team as well as spontaneity and is just plain fun. Please keep in mind: nothing planned, everything bared. Sounds impossible to do at first? You'll amaze yourself!

- Choose a number from 1 through 20.
- Find your number in the Stories That Have Never Been Told Before list, page 203.
- Write or type it at the top of the page.
- The first writer writes one word on the page.
- The second writer writes the next word.
- They continue, creating story elements and dialogue between the characters, one word at a time, switching characters and

telling the story—with NO pauses. No time to think. You see the word written, you begin the next word.

- Write until you have an organically created ending.

- Repeat this game, but this time, alternate whole sentences rather than words. Each person writes one sentence until you have a finished story. Sound impossible? Nah! Amaze yourself! Keep in mind: "Yes, and" is particularly important here.

- Feel free to play this over and over, adding certain things before you begin, like a genre you both want to create today.

Good job!

Now read this back, out loud! You made that!

EXAMPLE

Story Never Told Before: The Dragon of Altarezia

Writer 1: Once upon a time, in a castle plagued by tragedy, there lived, in chains, breeding anger, an ancient dragon.

Writer 2: She had scars covering the length of her body, and her fire, though long-extinguished, was today starting to spark once again.

Writer 1: The cause of this was clear as day—across the dungeon floor, clad in leather, was the very man who had captured her one hundred years before.

Writer 2: The Dragon of Altarezia slowly lifted her gaze.

Writer 1: A baby puff of smoke snorted from her nostrils.

OMG! What's going to happen? I almost couldn't stop myself.

> Remember: Plot is no more than footprints left in the snow after your characters have run by on their way to incredible destinations.
> —RAY BRADBURY

Plot and Structure

We're going to take some Ancient Writing Advice. Why not, when we're working in an art that has been around for thousands of years? In the first act, we will get our hero (or heroine) up a tree. In the second act we will throw rocks at our hero. In our third act, we will get that hero down.

This advice on writing has been attributed to so many writers, it's hard to keep track. There are versions by Steven Spielberg, George M. Cohan, Billy Wilder, Sol Saks—on and on. But we're gonna throw some rocks! We're going to do that, while playing a couple of games.

In a well-plotted story, ideally every scene becomes a turning point in which the values at stake swing from the positive to the negative or the negative to the positive, creating significant, but minor change in the characters' lives. In *Story*, Robert McKee defines and explains turning points well:

> Beats, changing patterns of human behavior, build scenes. Ideally, every scene becomes a Turning Point in which the values at stake swing from the positive to the negative or the negative to the positive, creating significant but minor change in their lives. A series of scenes build a sequence that culminates in a scene that has a moderate impact on the characters, turning or changing values

for better or worse to a greater degree than any scene. A series of sequences builds an act that climaxes in a scene that creates a major reversal in the characters' lives greater than any sequence accomplished.

Whew! When we are dealing with a story, part of the turning points I believe Robert McKee is talking about in *Story* is that we are letting our characters get some step closer to where they want to go and then we're pushing them back or keeping them from advancing in the next step. Thus creating suspense, interest, a little somethin' somethin'.

I want to share a game I love to teach, to watch, and to play so much I get itchy just thinking about it. Let's just start putting this character up a tree, toss some rocks, see what happens in the context of our story, our script. Oh, are we going to throw things at them! Oh ho ho!

#twistandshout

GAME: Raise the Stakes

Onstage, a scene gets started, and then intermittently the audience or another player offstage starts calling "Raise the stakes," which is exactly what it sounds like. In that very moment, no matter what is happening, something escalates. A good host will have this build until it's insanity, chaos, farcical, or all three! Think fire, death, pregnancy, blood, spit, fevers, tremors! Go big.

This isn't really a book on writing. It's a book on playing. It's a book for writers to explore and use, kinda like a creative gym membership. And plot is a great example of that. I want to play a game that can give you an entirely new plot that you didn't expect and probably wouldn't come up with without the pressure of a timer going off. You may or may not use it, but you will have some big, bold choices. Shazam!

WHY ON EARTH WOULD WE DO THIS?

We're doing this to see if we can spontaneously combust, of course! It's crazy-making, but it's also a delight. And the more you make bold choices in these games, playing around, the more it shows up in those stories that are so precious to us. Then we find ourselves doing things to our characters that we wouldn't have dreamed of. We're just practicing risk-taking and blowing things up. There's an old saying with actors that if you go into an audition and you're waaaay over the top, that's okay; that's better than walking in and no one can even hear what you're saying. Because the director can always pull you back. They at least know you can go *that* far. I think that's what this game does a little for us. Plus. Um. Fun!

It also gets you over that hump of being afraid of doing "bad" things to your characters in your real stories. We must torture them! Practicing this also helps to ensure that enough is happening and readers are more than interested—they are intrigued! Let's go!

- Grab yer timer.
- Set it to go off in a couple of minutes. We'll need that "snooze" function again so we can keep it going off every few minutes.
- Grab a scene of yours. Or start one, using some of the create-art-in-a-split-second tools we've got here.
- Choose a number from 1 through 40.
- Find your number in the Relationships list, page 201, and write the relationship at the top of the page. Give your characters some names.
- Choose a number from 1 through 50.
- Find your number in the Premises list, page 196. Write that premise at the top too.
- Set the timer for two minutes. Start writing a scene between these two characters.

- When the timer goes off, raise the stakes! Make something more exciting than what just happened happen.

- Reset the timer to now go off EVERY MINUTE.

- When it goes off again, you know what to do: raise the stakes, raise the roof, pull out all the stops!

- Keep raising the stakes until women are giving birth in a house on fire (actual brilliant scene played out by some teens in one of my classes—unreal!). Take it as far as you can by raising the stakes each time, higher and higher! Murder, mayhem, the formerly unthinkable. Go for it. Do that here.

- Do this at least six to eight times. More, if you dare! Mwah ha ha!

You writing machine, you!

QUICK TIP: Status Is Always Changing

In improv, status is a quick way to establish details about characters—one may be much higher status, boss, queen, older sibling, and so on—but this can shift throughout, so there's another fun element you can play with in setting up your characters and how they can change throughout the scene.

GAME: Motel

We are going to create a longer piece now. With three scenes, created and then each repeated. They all take place at a motel. Give yourself forty-five minutes to an hour for this game.

WHY ON EARTH WOULD WE DO THIS?

We do this to explore a setting and characters and heighten and build tension over a longer time period. An important thing that happens when working on a longer piece like this is the immersion in the creation. You may find you lose yourself in the writing. And what a far cry from agonizing over the blank page or stopping yourself from creating. If you've done all the games and exercises from earlier, this should be a nice buildup. You can also tailor this game for yourself once you've gone through it at least once. Change it from motel to upscale hotel. Or to anywhere in the world. A hostel in Bogotá. A military base in Cuba in the 1950s. Anywhere where multiple people would naturally intersect. With this game you can get as specific as you want later on. But for now, try and write without stopping, thinking, or judging for an even longer period. Let it all go and see who shows up at your motel today.

- Set the timer for five minutes.
- Do the game Paint the Scenery on a "motel" of your choice. It can be a nice tidy place or Creepsville—whatever you prefer, wherever your imagination takes you.
- Select three numbers from 1 through 40.
- Find your numbers in the Relationships list, page 201.
- Write all six characters at the top of the page. Give each a name and a short description.
- Set the timer again and for five minutes write a scene about one of the pairs. Establish the quality of their relationship, their goals, even some flaws, how they feel about this motel, their lives, and so on. Feel free to give any or all of the characters goals and flaws and specific quirks and descriptions. Add

some flavor, but don't get hung up trying to do total backstory on everyone for hours. Especially for the first time playing the game, you can keep it simple and just move through creating a longer piece.

- Repeat for the next scene, for the next two characters.

- Repeat once more for the final scene and characters. Now you have three scenes with three pairs, all taking place in the motel, and we understand, at least a bit, who the players all are.

- Our first round complete, let's move to the next level. On this second round of writing, we want to heighten what is going on with these characters. Remember Raise the Stakes? Don't be afraid to hurt these characters. Make some conflict.

- Set the timer for five minutes and write about that first pair again. Toss in some ways they are resisting their flaws, or things that are keeping them from their goals, raising those stakes along the way.

- Reset the timer again. Now give the second pair a similar treatment. Create some interaction with one or both of the other pairs of characters. Perhaps there's too much noise from one room, or smoke in a nonsmoking area, or they just run into each other at the ice machine.

- Reset the timer again for five minutes and write as the final pair. Heighten. Tension.

- When the timer goes off, reset it this last time for fifteen minutes.

- Write, bringing all these characters together in some way, in one particular location of the motel. Heighten what is happening with each of them and bring it to a climax! Remember, in choosing the location for the finale, you're not stuck with a parking lot with a light blinking on and off, although that would work, of course. There are lots of different kinds of motels out there. Choose something different. Maybe this one has a firepit, a creepy graveyard next to it, a hipster retro bar, a dumpy game room, a smelly laundry room, an upscale library lounge, a half-burnt-down vending room, an empty pool, a pond (with fowl), a kitschy gift shop, a basement in which to hide from the sudden hurricane—you get the idea.

- When the timer goes off, reset it for three minutes. Write the final resolution of what has transpired.

- Note: New characters might appear, or one or more of your characters might leave, die, disappear into the fog, and so on. The key is to keep the writing handwritten. You can always go back later and polish, adding in flaws and more descriptions like from Five Objects, Paint the Scenery, and other games.

Excellent!

GAME: Twists

Twists can really make a story stand out. Ummm, hello—mother of all twists in *Sharp Objects, The Sixth Sense, The Crying Game,* and the like—but great sketches and funny commercials have them too, as does just about every good stand-up comedy joke. It's misdirection and surprise—nestled together in a way that feels natural, not shoe-horned in—that can really can get the audience going. Yeah, twist and shout! In this game, you'll start out writing a scene about two characters, and then it will turn out that their circumstances—even who they are—are the opposite of what they seem!

WHY ON EARTH WOULD WE DO THIS?

Readers love surprises! Keep doing this until it is absolutely absurd. And who knows? Maybe you'll even find one you want to keep or develop for real, despite its seeming ridiculous in the beginning . . . or the end. You might find this goes to such an unbelievable place that you would never actually use it. Or maybe you would. Or maybe there's something in the middle there that blew your mind. The point is that you're stretching where you are willing to go and trying something new. That can only be a good thing, because you know you can always reel things back in. But you can't always make an explosion happen if you've never thought about doing things differently. Surprise yourself.

- Set your timer to go off every minute.
- Choose a number from 1 through 40.
- Find your number in the Relationships list, page 201.
- Choose a dramatic place for these two to be today.
- Start writing a scene between these two.
- Every time the timer goes off, change something to be the opposite of what it was before. Keep building, letting each thing that was different be bigger than the last thing when the timer went off, so you're also heightening.
- Write until your head pops off.

Wahoooo! You did it!

EXAMPLE

Were your characters at a hotel? Now it actually turns out to be a secret prison!

Was the first date going well? It actually turned out that they both couldn't wait to get away from each other.

Was your main character a sex-crazed boy? Now it turns out he's actually, secretly a virgin!

Was your other character a human girl? It turns out she's actually an alien placed on earth to have sex with the boy, just for research!

Was the grandmotherly character who was answering the phones at her son's company as sweet and kind as she seemed? Or was she really the mastermind behind the downfall of the entire corporation?

Mwah ha ha!

GAME: Good/Bad/Worst/Fixed

Conflict is important in storytelling. And early improvisational theater had plenty of it. Even if there were laughs in commedia dell'arte, people were being cheated on, lied to, chased.

In working with Gary Austin and other directors, I learned just how valuable and malleable the art truly is. We can create heavy, serious moments, full of intense conflicts and flaws given to each character; sometimes it is as simple as one character wants something so badly and the other character is directed to not give in. And then the scene is played out, discoveries are made, and the final piece is stronger because of this conflict, overcome or not.

This game gives us opportunities to explore our scripts and our characters through conflicts. We're going to put your characters through some paces and, like we did in Raise the Stakes, we're going to stoke the fire of conflict with heightening every few minutes. This is also, in its simplicity, a not-too-shabby story arc that takes about fifteen minutes. You might just get an actual short story that you love out of this. If you sell this baby, let me know.

WHY ON EARTH WOULD WE DO THIS?

This big twist on an improv game gives us a simple way to practice throwing rocks at our hero in the tree, then getting him down. Feel free to try this with a project you've had in your back pocket, to see what other kinds of trouble you can get your characters in and out of. You can do this as an overview of an entire script or just get into one scene. There's a lot of room to develop some funny, scary stuff very quickly here.

- Set the timer for five minutes.
- Choose a number from 1 through 100 for a protagonist, a number from 1 through 50 for an antagonist, and a number from 1 through 50 for a premise.
- Find your numbers in their respective lists, pages 198, 187, and 196.

- Write a scene establishing these two people and their situation.

- The first time the timer goes off, we should have a lot established. Reset the timer for two minutes. Now, something **good** happens to our main character.

- When it goes off next, something **bad** happens to your protagonist. Reset the timer for two minutes.

- This third time, something **worse** happens to your protagonist. Reset the timer once again for a final four minutes.

- The fourth time, write a **fix**. Whatever the trouble was, resolve it in some way.

Well, look atchoo!

QUICK TIP: Warm Up

Get the blood moving. Every class or show in improv starts with a warm-up. Why not do this for your writing? Some days you may want to be very centered, and there are games to do this, but other times, like right before a big writing day with a big, challenging section, you may want to breakdance. Yeah, I said that. You could also do a hundred jumping jacks. The idea is, not only are we shaking up how ideas come to us and the way we get them down on paper, but we're also getting new ways of moving into our body, some action. Then we can write that action scene!

Style is to forget all styles.
—JULES RENARD

Genres

You can create as many genres or styles as you like by mixing exist-ing ones. Or you can stay in one particular lane all the time. What's fun about genres is that each one has its own laws in place. People in a horror film act a certain way, and we all expect certain things to happen. And there are varying degrees of horror as well. You can go as campy or real-istic, as jump-scare or creepy mind-bending as you like.

What I love about genre is that it helps rein in the story a little, gives it some parameters. And of course, you can cross and blend those lines too. Hey, we're seeding the future of entertainment with our cross-pollinating ideas. I have a list in the back of the book, and you can always combine some to make your own if that's more to your liking.

Knowing your genre strengths is like knowing how to use your super-powers for good. And exploring other genres outside of what you normally write and enjoy is more stretching of your creativity and imagination. Some ideas need to be explored in a different genre. Sometimes you can deliver a message about something heavy, important, and relevant in a comedy that you could never, ever do elsewhere.

Exploring, understanding, and writing in other genres helps us understand people and characters better. In doing improv, part of the crazy-scary goodness of it comes from being asked to do something onstage that you've never done before—in front of people. And there is tremendous growth in working within an area of art that you are not that familiar with. When you're asked to create, on the spot, a scene from a rom-com, it may not be a genre you watch, like, or know much about, but you pull from every corner of your brain anything you can think of that has anything to do with romantic comedies. And you create from there. And yes, sometimes what comes out is unique, because it's you and you are so, so unique, and sometimes it doesn't hardly make any sense. But you tried. And in trying, we grow.

All this to say, check out another corner of literature, film, theater. See what they're doing over there. See if you can make something the world has never seen before.

#genretime

GAME: Genre Swap

Here is a game with revolving categories to push and pull and play with. This game is a tool for writers to take some of their work and see how it translates in another arena—potentially they may find they newly have a great children's book or an unexpected thriller.

Part of the fun of playing or watching this game onstage is the switching of the actors into each style, whether the audience calls out "Southern Gothic!" "Western!" or "Sci-Fi!" For us, we're just going to see if a script that we've got lying around might be more interesting to us (or our agents) if we try on some different genres, like trying on a new pair of shoes. A different pair of shoes can totally change the portrayal of a character, unbelievably, and a switch in genre can completely change a story or script.

WHY ON EARTH WOULD WE DO THIS?

Who knows? You might just find that you have a whole new story to pitch. If you don't have something you've already written, grab a story in the public domain and use that. You might end up with a great pitch for an updated fairy tale or kids' book. The possibilities are infinite. How many times can I say that? Soooo many! Try another genre, and potentially discover new life for an old story you didn't quite know what to do with before.

- Pick a script or short story of yours or one that is in the public domain. I've included a short Public Domain Stories list, page 200. Choose a number from 1 through 10 if you want to try one of those classics.

- Get a pen to write in the margins or "save as" a new title if you're working digitally.

- Select one pivotal scene in your story or script.

- Choose a new genre for it from the Genres list, page 192.

- Set the timer for five minutes.

- Adapt it to the conventions of the genre.

- Write in first or third person, but even though it may be a new genre for you, don't think, just commit, and write like the wind!

Unstoppable!

GAME: Movie-Making Machine

Remember when we played Ad Agency and you pitched a movie idea? We're going to do it again, now that we've had many opportunities to exercise the important muscle of agreement. Again, you'll select a made-up movie (or series) title from the provided list (or make up your own movie title). You're again going to pitch it to imaginary film/television executives, but this time you will also choose the genre and use whatever information you have to sell this thing!

WHY ON EARTH WOULD WE DO THIS?

We're practicing coming up with more and more ideas and letting them all exist at once. There's no reason to judge, because
it's all made up. It doesn't exist. Don't let yourself start thinking or
hesitating—this is silly and freeing and all about agreeing with the
FIRST thing you think of and adding to it!

- Choose a number from 1 through 25.
- Find your number in the Movies That Have Not Been Made . . .
  Yet! list, page 195.
- Write the title at the top of the page.
- Say the title out loud.
- Under the title, write the first genre that springs to mind
  (Western, animation, rom-com, thriller, and so on).
- If nothing jumps to mind, check the Genres list, page 192.
- Set the timer for five minutes.
- Become a powerful creative writer with many similar beloved
  movies in this genre. Let the ideas flow, and pitch this movie!
- If any come to mind quickly, add real or made-up celebrities
  of this genre—or imagine if you got a star to cross over from a
  genre they've stuck with for their entire career! Could be a sell-
  ing point.
- Remember to start each sentence by agreeing and adding info!
  "Yes . . . and!"
- Write until the timer goes off.
- If you didn't do so on this round, I would love for you to try the
  game again with your own made-up title.

Yah! Yah! YAH!

GAME: Soap Opera

Now for a game that is its own genre. It's like Raise the Stakes from our chapter on plot. Get ready to get a little, oh, I don't know (hand across forehead; deep sigh)—dramatic!

Take any scene you've written here or outside of these reindeer games. Start going through each beat. Wherever you can, add a twist a la the Soap Opera genre. Keep doing this until it is absolutely absurd. Who knows, maybe you'll even find one you want to keep or develop for real, despite its seeming ridiculous in the beginning.

WHY ON EARTH WOULD WE DO THIS?

The more we take risks while playing around, the more challenges we give our characters, the bolder we get in our writing, and that's great, idn't it? Idn't it?

Take some risks and take it faaaaarther than you normally would. You just may find the next twist or heightened move that you were looking for. You can also just have some fun. There is a lot of love out there for soaps; that's why even when we think they're going away, they're still clinging, like Bo and Hope, to each other! On the side of a building. While on fire. And giving birth.

- Set your timer to go off every two minutes, or every minute and a half (adjust these slightly for your typing speed).
- Choose a number from 1 through 40.
- Find your number in the Relationship list, page 201.
- Choose a dramatic place for these two to be today.
- Start writing a scene between these two.
- Every time the timer goes off, there must be a slap or a kiss.
- Write until your head pops off.

Put yer head back on, ya maniac!

Pick a theme and work it to exhaustion . . .
the subject must be something you
truly love or truly hate.
—DOROTHEA LANGE

Theme

One of my favorite quotes ever about writing—comedy, specifically, though I do think it completely holds up in drama too—is what Sol Saks says in *Funny Business: The Craft of Comedy Writing*: "Style (and originality perhaps) is really simple honesty. No one is exactly like you. No one feels exactly as you do. So . . . if you write with integrity, nothing will be exactly like it and there's your originality and style. Comedy, written with graceful ease, is always readable, usually simple, and most always honest. . . . Style can be called the personality of your writing, and, like your own personality, it becomes awkward and dishonest if you are self-conscious about it."

What are you, the writer, saying with your piece? What do you want to convey? Where do you want to go, to be taken? It could be simple or complex, but having an idea of this, loose or concrete, is helpful in shaping not just this story, but your voice as a writer. Onstage, I often find that I set out to have a lot of scenes that also somehow express the way I try to live life: joyful, fun, inventive, and connecting deeply to the person(s) in the scene with me. This sort of happens naturally. And I always want to play a lot of varied characters, just like in life. I like to be different ways with different people I care about. With some I like to laugh heartily and dance wildly; with others, I just want to sit and look at the stars and maybe ponder the universe and what is real. It might sound, well, however it sounds—but that's me, and I just want to express myself truthfully in life, on the stage, and on the page.

As an actress, this is the most make-or-break point for me in deciding to involve myself in a script. I was recently offered a role in a comedy-horror film. It was a lead role, and I was excited at first, but when I looked closer at the script, not only was the comedy not my style, but there was no message. It was devoid of a theme and didn't seem to be saying anything except one kinda gross thing. I passed and never looked back. This aspect of story alone makes it easy for agents, editors, directors, and other collaborators to make their decision on whether to involve themselves in a project. Whatever theme or message you choose, always be true to yourself. You'll get the people who are right for your project if you are really saying something that you mean.

Lesson. Moral. Point of the story. Universal idea. Message. Different words to cover theme. What is this piece of art saying to the world? Is it glorifying violence or creating a negative body image? I say, "no thank you." Is it uplifting or simply shining a spotlight on an injustice? Sign me up.

The theme of each piece you write is incredibly personal. You may think about it a lot; it may be what got you writing. It may be something that comes out naturally without any thought at all. Of course, additional messages that weren't even intended in a story can be found, just like in a painting, but let's keep it simple. It doesn't have to be complicated, but choosing a meaning or message can be fun, can change, can be transcendent.

This next game is an opportunity to consciously insert a message into one of our character's monologues in two ways: obvious and subtle. Each has its place, and it's good to be able to do both.

#thethemeisthething

GAME: Message in a Monologue

We're going to write once again with a strong point of view, that of your protagonist. And we're going to write them straight up, stating a strong message to whomever they are speaking. We are going to be very obvious in the first round and then write a second piece, choosing a more subtle way to say the same thing.

WHY ON EARTH WOULD WE DO THIS?

This game is helpful if you often struggle with being subtle in your message. No one wants to be hit over the head repeatedly with what you're trying to say. This game is also helpful if your struggle is being *too* subtle, and you repeatedly get feedback that your message didn't come through as intended, then *you* reverse the game order, so the second time you write the piece, the message is *more* obvious.

Using this, we can discover more obvious *and* more subtle ways to say the same thing.

- Choose a number from 1 through 100.
- Find your number in the Protagonists list, page 198.
- Select the corresponding message from the Themes list, page 205.
- Set the timer for five minutes.
- In character, create a monologue (or scene) that directly states that message. Actually, use the same words from the chosen theme.
- Reset the timer for five minutes.
- Write a second monologue, this one communicating the message but without using the words directly.

I hear ya!

GAME: Twist of Theme

We're going to reimagine a piece of art in a new way. We're going to change its original meaning or intention in some small or large way.

WHY ON EARTH WOULD WE DO THIS?

It's just more opportunity to spend playing around with one of the most powerful reasons to even be an artist. What are you really trying to say? Can you say it another way? Is there a secondary message or theme?

This is also great practice for adapting a piece and letting your own voice and purpose for writing that piece shine through. There is so much incredible work out there in the public domain that isn't as easily accessible to today's audiences, perhaps because of language or at first not seeming as relevant, but you can shed new light; you can heighten a message or bring your own interpretation alive!

- Select a scene from one of the Public Domain Stories, page 200, or one of your scripts, or even a play on your shelf—any story will do, and you can definitely use your own. Spend a couple of minutes reading it.
- Select a message from the Themes list, page 205.
- Write that theme at the top of the page.
- Set the timer for five minutes.
- With that scene and this new theme in mind, start writing your own version of that short piece.

Good job!

> Rewriting is when writing really gets to be
> fun. . . . In baseball you only get three swings
> and you're out. In rewriting, you get almost as
> many swings as you want and you know, sooner
> or later, you'll hit the ball.
> —NEIL SIMON

Editing

We edit in improv. We do it from the back line of the theater or on the sidelines, watching the scene being played out for the audience, ready to jump in and help or build momentum or change the rhythm—whatever we instinctually feel is needed in this moment. We either stay there, out of that way, or we leap forward, not turning back (everyone's looking at you), and we edit. But we don't get much—scratch that, *any*—chance to rewrite a scene. Not during that same show.

This game is as close as we get to it. And it is a ridiculous amount of fun. **#editeverything**

QUICK TIP: Go On Your Own Way

Now that you're whizzing around the games and having some fun, if you find you used the lists a lot, go ahead and make your own. Set the timer for a few minutes and create your own list for the games you are playing the most, or all of them, *or* ask for one from a stranger. Now there's a special moment!

GAME: Countdown or 5, 2, 1, :30, :15

We're going to write a scene based on a premise or headline or your own idea. Woo hoo! Then we're going to rewrite it in shorter and shorter increments of time. Get ready for a hand cramp.

WHY ON EARTH WOULD WE DO THIS?

It really works out the essentials of what's happening, doesn't it? It's also a good opportunity to sweat a little. I know I do when playing this. Did I mention fun?

- Select either a premise or a headline from the Premises or Headlines lists, page 196 or 193, or from your own files or from today's news.
- Select a setting from the Settings list, page 201. Make sure the setting makes sense; if it doesn't, just pick one that does.
- Choose either your own character or a protagonist on page 198.
- Select either an antagonist or a supporting player from those lists, page 187 or 204, or use your own.
- Set the timer for five minutes.
- Write the scene.
- Set the time again and rewrite it in two minutes, capturing the most important elements.
- Repeat again, but in one minute.
- Thirty seconds.
- Fifteen seconds.

Good stuff!

Write, rewrite, rinse, repeat.

Afterword: Living with These Games

These rules, this book, is just a starting point. People who do improv do it for life. Other people will take a class and say they tried that thing once, in college, it was fun, but the next opportunity, there was a party to attend and life got distracting, and . . . well, you know. It was a thing. It was cool. But whatever.

But the people who *really* do improv? They know the life- and career-changing benefits. The concerted efforts make you a better human: How? Well, let's take a look. Someone who practices the rules and games of improvisation starts to become a very special person indeed. It can help you

- Find ways to agree with people.
- Always be able to continue the conversation with anyone.
- Be and stay present.
- Trust that you are not making mistakes, but constantly daring greatly.
- Really hear what others are saying, rather than planning what you will say next.
- Commit fully and know what it feels like to be the kind of person, artist, everything you desire to be.
- Be very specific, and make choices that surprise, pop, and crackle.

- Have intention in your words, your work.
- Be less judge-y of others and yourself.
- Become an enthusiastic monster of wonderfulness.

I strongly encourage you to continue traveling the improvisor's path. We have a language of our own, and we want everyone to learn it, for it is universal, it is generous, it is colorful, and it is creative beyond measure.

Make World and Project-Specific Lists

To continue using these games and do with improv what has been done with improv for thousands of years (adjust it), go ahead and make lists that you can use throughout a project. For example, if you're creating a fantasy series and you want to spend a few minutes a day working on it—discovering, exploring, getting out of your head—make a list for that world. You can title all the lists for this fantasy project. You'll get even more mileage.

EXAMPLE:

Your new passion project is called the Myths of Myradooor. You create a "Myths of Myradooor Objects" list to play all the object games with. The objects could be already known to you from your research and world-building, or they could be written gibberish-style, quickly (use a timer!?) and their use decided later—or it could be a mix of these two. You can do the same for any and all applicable lists. "The Protagonists of Myradooor," "The Antagonists of Myradooor," "The Settings of Myradooor." You can even create new games. You are so welcome to do what I've done and make amendments to warm-ups and games for your own project- and character-specific purposes. And then you can play, play, play in your own world, deepening not only your own experience, but the reader's too.

That's it, new friends. Come back and revisit this when you want to come up with new ideas, when you feel stuck, when you're staring at a blank page. Improv is here for you. Improv is yours.

Go forth and play!

#improviseimprov

Acknowledgments

I am so grateful to so many for their help and support in this creation.

Firstly, Lisa Westmoreland at Ten Speed Press for picking up what I was putting down. I am so very, truly grateful to her. As creatives, we know when we throw spaghetti at the wall, some stringy bits stick, and some fall limply to the floor. The people who also see this oh, so personal thing you are lobbing out there into the world and who take turns pelting it and pushing it and changing it with you—they're sometimes the only thing keeping you going with the idea keeping you up at night. Lisa made this book possible. She believed in the ideas and organized them and then she reined in the wild horses of possibility to become racers ready to take you wherever you want to go. Secondly, Gordon Warnock, my agent at Fuse Literary. From the second our lives intersected, so much has aligned in mine. Oh, oh the joy of having professionals in publishing travel the road with you.

I also want to thank all the professional writers bringing their experience, and total beginners dabbling who played these games to help me, especially friends: Matt O'Connell, Kate Winslet, Cynthia Levin, Anna and Michael Rann, and Dave Cain.

I can remember exactly where I was standing when the idea for this whole thing started sprawling out. It was at Comic Con, of all places, talking with Melessa Sargent of Scriptwriters Network about doing a workshop at CBS on improv for writers.

I owe a lot to divine connections and the support of the writing community at large. Being a part of the Deadline Junkies was a big chunk of my movement forward. Special thanks to Geena Davis and her Institute for lighting a writing fire within me.

There are so many giants of drama, improv, comedy, and writing instruction from whom I've learned so much: Gary Austin, my very first improv teacher, who helped me understand that improvisation can be anything you want it to be, anything you need it to be. Carol Kennedy, who, in high school, let me teach improv for the first time to our drama club and who taught me there are no small parts, only small actors. She gave me freedom in the form of performance wings. The Lembecks, for creating a space to be very, very creative and expressive. My training and shows in sketch and improv at UCBNY and LA and Amy Poehler, in particular, for pushing the boundaries of the art. My teachers at iO West: Craig Cackowski, for being one of the best teachers I have ever studied with, and Holly Laurent, for her warmth and philosophy. Gene Frankel, legendary Broadway director, who taught me to throw spaghetti at the wall and encouraged me to bring my character monologues into classes in classics, my strange characters a little out of place against the Blanches and Stellas, the Juliets and queens—nonetheless, my first place to bring in my written work. Chris Smith, who would understand in seconds what each student or scene needed. I was dumbfounded at how he and teachers like Gary and Craig could do that. Robert McKee, for breaking story down in a way that turned the lightbulb on for me.

Every child or adult who ever played these games with me, especially the kids who taught me what improvisation really is and how tailoring the games for their individual needs makes the games and concepts invaluable. Yes, I am saying if you get something out if this—kids are totally behind it. Those mad geniuses. Especially Matt and Matthew in Santa Clarita; thank you for being geniuses at something new and for always committing.

So grateful to my Groundlings friend, Nicole Salandra Tupper, for being the best kind of friend in improv and in life and for sharing her parents, Tessa and Gene, with me.

I'm grateful to my mom, brother, aunts, uncles, and grandparents for their support—it's always meant more than I could ever say.

An extra-special thanks to childhood best friends: Bobbie Jo, who set the bar for friendship extraordinarily high and would always, always play, explore, laugh, and take our silliness even farther—my BFF, my original improv partner. Diane Elizabeth, who changed the course of my life with her wisdom, encouragement, calm, goodness, and true-blue friendship and continues to be a voice in my head.

Lastly, but you know how it goes, *certainly* not least, my husband, Phillip Mosness, who played these games with me too (oh, so much fun!) and came up with stories that amazed and entertained me. His smart suggestions and generosity of time and care helped this book come to fruition. He was the first to inspire and gently push me to share this, believing in it and sensing the power and possibility of it right away. On the spot. Without thinking. A natural improvisor! To me, the best kind of person to be, the best kind of partner to have. The very best.

Thank you!

Appendix: Lists

Personally, I love randomness, random things, the unusual popping up. One of the main reasons people laugh is surprise, so these lists will keep you on your toes, discovering, just by following the bread crumbs, as you do each game in the book.

I recommend making your own lists that cover your go-tos, or maybe put a whole lot of new characters you might not have thought of right away up front in your lobes. To mix it up. When you're looking for ideas, the dictionary is great. Magazines too. I was once in improv class and the teacher, when she wanted a suggestion, would open a magazine at random and say things like, "You're in a laundromat—go!" Other than that, I'm improvising, just making this all up. You can do that for yourself too, for the genres you like to work in, the types of characters you like to "cast" in your movies—write additional lists—stick 'em in here or create a notebook or file full of 'em. You'll never be in need of a story idea again! The real trick is to just start. These will assist with the exercises and are frequently referenced throughout the text.

AGES

1. Infant
2. Toddler
3. Age three
4. Age five
5. Age six
6. Age seven
7. Age nine
8. Tween
9. Age fourteen
10. Age sixteen
11. Age eighteen
12. Age twenty
13. Age twenty-one
14. Age twenty-five
15. Age twenty-eight
16. Age thirty
17. Age thirty-five
18. Age forty
19. Age forty-five
20. Age fifty
21. Age fifty-five
22. Age sixty
23. Age sixty-five
24. Age seventy
25. Age seventy-five
26. Age eighty
27. Age eighty-five
28. Age ninety
29. Age ninety-five
30. Age 100
31. Age 105
32. Age 110
33. Age 120
34. Age 150
35. Age 200
36. Age 300
37. Age 500
38. Age 1,000
39. Age 2,000
40. Age 10,000
41. _____

ANIMALS

1. Kitten
2. Turtle
3. Orangutan
4. Chinchilla
5. Lion
6. Giraffe
7. Alpaca
8. Zebra
9. Opossum
10. Raccoon
11. Aardvark
12. Kangaroo
13. Wolf
14. Jaguar
15. Panda
16. Penguin
17. Baboon
18. Gorilla
19. Snake
20. Dolphin
21. Shark
22. Octopus
23. Grizzly bear
24. Dog
25. Sloth
26. Tarantula
27. Butterfly
28. Polar bear
29. Cockroach
30. Puffin
31. Duck
32. Chicken
33. Goat
34. Llama
35. Sheep
36. Deer
37. Rabbit
38. Cheetah
39. Armadillo
40. Crocodile
41. Boa constrictor
42. Eagle
43. Buzzard
44. Blue Jay
45. Ostrich
46. Flying fish
47. Squirrel
48. Pterodactyl
49. Elephant
50. Hippopotamus
51. _____

ANTAGONISTS

1. Unfriendly pariah—social outcast
2. Antagonistic barista
3. Parasitic poker champion
4. Dangerous grocer
5. Possessed business partner
6. Obsessed stalker
7. Power-hungry politician
8. Impulsive convict
9. Abusive parent
10. Volatile stranger
11. Insistent IRS auditor
12. Alcoholic sibling
13. Terse meter-maid/man
14. Distant grandparent
15. Coercive drill sergeant
16. Smug doctor
17. Vindictive associate
18. Argumentative thief
19. Plastic (everything on the surface) friend
20. Disorderly line-cook
21. Daring bully
22. Alcoholic gold-digger
23. Intolerable alien
24. Meddling virtual assistant
25. Sinister driver
26. Rigid monster
27. Careful snake
28. Moody stunt person
29. Unsociable servant
30. Melancholic beggar
31. Conniving congressperson
32. Unfaithful spouse
33. Vibrant vampire
34. Relentless salesperson
35. Calm zombie
36. Driven sociopath
37. Precise henchman
38. Mocking thief
39. Desperate traitor
40. Lost child
41. Creepy crossing guard
42. Broken wizard
43. Vulgar landlord
44. Wasteful apartment manager
45. Sneaky mummy
46. Close-talking pyromaniac
47. Patient serial killer
48. Clever mortician
49. Shrewd terrorist
50. Sharp psychic
51. _____

EMOTIONS

1. Joyful
2. Hateful
3. Happy
4. Jealous
5. Enraged
6. Shy
7. Irate
8. Loving
9. Numb
10. Scared
11. Lustful
12. Enraptured
13. Angst-ridden
14. Grieving
15. Blissful
16. Disgusted
17. Annoyed
18. Confused
19. Exasperated
20. Frustrated
21. Terrified
22. Envious
23. Terrific
24. Thankful
25. Unhappy
26. Weepy
27. Humiliated
28. Mortified
29. Embarrassed
30. Lost
31. Empty
32. Worn
33. Contented
34. Desperate
35. Dazed
36. Ambivalent

37. Nervous
38. Stressed
39. Despondent
40. Disappointed
41. Disillusioned
42. Empathetic
43. Eager
44. Satisfied
45. Bashful
46. Sympathetic
47. Thrilled
48. Powerful
49. Glorious
50. Used
51. Awestruck
52. Compassionate
53. Determined
54. Active
55. Curious
56. Purposeful
57. Prideful
58. Ashamed
59. Guilty
60. Hostile
61. Contentious
62. Covetous
63. Euphoric
64. Hopeful
65. Energized
66. Surprised
67. Shocked
68. Grumpy
69. Agitated
70. Belligerent
71. Peaceful
72. Calm
73. Overwhelmed
74. Panicked

75. Respected
76. Motivated
77. Restless
78. Worried
79. Perplexed
80. Boxed In
81. Burdened
82. Exposed
83. Weak
84. Listless
85. Depressed
86. Crushed
87. Dejected
88. Indifferent
89. Withdrawn
90. Disheartened
91. Heartbroken
92. Heavyhearted
93. Lighthearted
94. Wrecked
95. Wretched
96. Mad
97. Powerful
98. Cherished
99. Nurturing
100. Present
101. Serene
102. Creative
103. Amused
104. Helpless
105. Submissive
106. Insecure
107. Bewildered
108. Insignificant
109. Inadequate
110. Daring
111. Fascinated
112. Sensuous

113. Wild
114. Optimistic
115. Pumped!
116. Goofy
117. Thrilled
118. Silly
119. Worthy
120. Untouchable
121. Vulnerable
122. Meek
123. Appreciative
124. Important
125. Faithful
126. Disingenuous
127. Discerning
128. Manipulative
129. Enigmatic
130. Intuitive
131. Destructive
132. Pensive
133. Volatile
134. Unpredictable
135. Bored
136. Isolated
137. Inferior
138. Remorseful
139. Rebellious
140. Hurt
141. Selfish
142. Critical
143. Skeptical
144. Disrespected
145. Vengeful
146. Timid
147. Intolerant
148. Mournful
149. Wary
150. Defensive
151. _____

ENDOWMENTS

1. Chronically cannot get enough oxygen
2. Obese
3. Occluded vision
4. Brittle bones
5. Offensive, uncontrollable body odor
6. Pregnancy
7. Gigantism
8. Stunted growth
9. Gout
10. Osteoporosis
11. Stomach cancer
12. Throat cancer
13. Asthma
14. Halitosis
15. Swollen joints
16. Hangnail
17. Blisters on the feet
18. Ripped, extremely muscular
19. Healthy, physically fit
20. Fragile
21. Pale
22. Skin cancer
23. Tanned, healthy glow
24. Generally weak
25. Excessive testosterone
26. Flabby
27. Pallid, lacking vitality
28. Vibrant, full of vitality
29. Average in every way
30. Heart palpitations
31. Palsy-complete or partial muscle paralysis
32. Auto-immune disorder
33. Full of parasites
34. Inebriated
35. Tipsy
36. Vertigo
37. Thyroid condition
38. Balding
39. 20/20 vision
40. Lazy eye
41. Steel rods in back
42. One leg shorter than the other
43. Brain tumor
44. Extreme height
45. Ulcers
46. Chronic acne
47. Webbed feet
48. Anemia
49. Narcolepsy
50. Excessive estrogen
51. _____

FLAWS

1. They have this feeling they are always being watched and followed. Extreme paranoia. But they won't admit they have a problem and get professional help.
2. They believe life is better high. And they won't face up to the fact that they have an addiction.
3. They believe a drink will make things better. So they don't address their real problems on a deeper level.
4. They believe they have to be perfect and do everything perfectly. They don't realize that this keeps them at a "safe" distance from messy, real human relationships.
5. They have an unusually high opinion of themselves and their appearance and skills. They are blind to their flaws.
6. They feel they don't have any worth, don't deserve anything.
7. They believe they will always be left behind by everyone they care about. They don't realize they are not engaging in life and they have something valuable to offer.
8. They believe they are unlucky and will ruin and break

everything that is good or going well. They don't realize they have the agency to enact change.

9. They do not believe anyone should ever trust them because they will turn on them. They don't realize they have an inner goodness beneath their self-protective shell.

10. They believe it would have been better if they had never been born. They don't realize they have the power to do good in the world.

11. They believe they are too old. They don't realize that they still have much life left to live.

12. They believe they are too young. They do not yet realize that their experiences have given them a wisdom they can tap into.

13. They believe they are weak, incapable of ever fighting back or speaking up for what they believe. They need to discover their inner strength.

14. They believe they are a victim and will always be a target for others. They need to realize they have what it takes to stand up for themselves.

15. They believe they don't have enough and there will never be enough—resources are scarce. They need to learn how to dream up hopes and fight for them.

16. They believe they are always at a disadvantage, they are the underdog. They need to become empowered to lose the chip on their shoulder.

17. They believe they are a deity— have delusions of grandeur. They need to come down to earth.

18. They believe it is their job to point out issues or problems with others, that people won't learn otherwise; they enjoy causing trouble for others, thinking they are creating opportunities for others to have growth. They need to learn the limits of radical honesty and the power of empathy.

19. They believe they have been wronged continuously throughout life. They need to learn how to take responsibility for their own future.

20. They have an irrational belief in astrology and fate; superstition gets in the way of their making rational choices. They need to learn that fate is what they make of it.

21. They believe everyone else owes them something. They need to learn to rely on themselves.

22. They believe they will never change and there is no point in trying. They need to learn how to grow.

23. They have been spoiled since childhood and feel that they have the right to anything they want—they certainly don't have to work for it or earn anything. They need to learn the fulfillment of accomplishing things for themselves.

24. They believe no one will ever love them. They need to learn self-worth.

25. They overdramatize everything in their life; every little thing that happens is blown out of proportion and made into a big event or production. They need to gain perspective.

26. They believe if they get something, someone else will take it away. They need to learn how to trust.

27. They believe that if someone does love them, they will eventually leave them. They need to learn how to appreciate the current moment for what it is.

28. They believe they must stand by their friends and family no matter what they do or who they hurt; family is everything. They need to find their own moral compass.

29. They believe they have all the answers, and all the people around them are a bunch of idiots. They need to learn to acknowledge others' strengths.

30. They believe they deserve wealth and that money is the most important thing in life. They need to learn what's really valuable in life.

31. They believe their suffering will be worthwhile and are willing to sacrifice themselves for a good cause. They need to replace their martyrdom with a healthier way of being.

32. They believe disease is everywhere and are unwilling to connect physically or emotionally with others to keep themselves safe. They need to break down those walls to live a full life.

33. They believe they can seduce anyone and that sexual power over others is more important than anything else. They need to learn how to truly connect.

34. They feel that everyone around them is a joke and if they mock them subtly, perhaps they will all wake up. They need to learn how to value others.

35. They believe being strict and disciplined is the only way to live life, and any lenience in even small matters is unacceptable. They need to learn to appreciate the unpredictable.

36. They believe if they can't protect others, their life is pointless. They need to learn that they can only do their best.

37. They have such a strong need to succeed that any kind of failure is unacceptable and demoralizing. They need to become comfortable with their imperfections.

38. They believe it is their job to put people in their place and control them. They need to learn they can only control themselves.

39. They feel they have a right to know every little and big thing that is going on with everyone in their life, even if it annoys them. They need to learn to be less controlling and more empathetic and open.

40. They don't believe that any harm can ever come to them. They need to replace their naïveté with streetwise experience.

41. They have no interest in "growing up" or need to do so; they enjoy playing pranks and "getting" people. They need to gain some maturity.

42. They tell everything like it is; no filtering of the harsh truth. They need to learn that not everyone can handle the truth and that softening the truth can be a necessary kindness.

43. They believe telling people the truth only hurts their feelings, and getting creative and embellishing stories makes people like them more. They need to learn how to be honest with others and themselves.

44. They believe being dominant over others is the most important power play that can be made, and they are willing to dominate everyone they cross paths with. They need to learn that rewarding human relationships are about give and take.

45. They believe people are always cheating them. They need to learn how to trust.

46. They believe there is no good in the world. They need to learn how to see the glass half full.

47. They believe it is their job to fix other people's problems, even if no one asks them to; it's up to them to help those who can't help themselves. They need to learn to focus on fixing their own problems first.

48. They believe they are someone else's responsibility and do not have to take care of themselves; someone else will look after them. They need to build self-reliance.

49. They believe everyone should be under their control and do as they ask. They need to learn how to go with the flow and let others be who they are.

50. They believe they will never be free; that everyone who wants to be in a relationship with them is trying to cage them. They need to learn how to be in a healthy relationship.

51. _____
_____
_____

GENRES (FILM, TV, LITERATURE)

1. Comedy
2. Drama
3. Romantic Comedy
4. Dramedy
5. Bromedy
6. Historical Fiction
7. Biopic or Biographical Fiction
8. Period Piece
9. Western
10. Science Fiction
11. Suspense/Thriller
12. Documentary
13. Mockumentary
14. Romance
15. Satire
16. Parody
17. Spoof
18. Tragedy
19. Tragicomedy
20. Fantasy
21. Mythology
22. Adventure
23. Mystery
24. Dystopian
25. Crime/Detective
26. Musical
27. Soap Opera
28. Animation
29. Teen Drama
30. Teen Comedy
31. Children's
32. Fairy Tale
33. Fable
34. Classic
35. Fanfiction
36. _____

HEADLINES

1. They Fell in Love at Five Years Old; See Them 20 Years Later
2. World's Oldest Person Dies at 117
3. Do You Come From Royal Blood? Your Last Name May Tell You
4. "Golden" Kitten Saves Debt-Laden Animal Shelter
5. Drive-by Shooters Targeted Wrong Home
6. 3-Legged Dog Finally Gets a Taste of Freedom
7. Beauty Queen Stood Her Ground with a Bat
8. 3D Printing Technology Brings Bionic Eye One Step Closer
9. School Mistakenly Sends 7-Year-Old Home with Wrong Parent
10. Football Teams Meet in a Duel of the Disappointed
11. Advocates Return Wild Horses to Herd
12. Girl Bites Into Nail in Halloween Candy
13. 5 Ways to Get Rid of Earworms
14. How a Catastrophic Cosmic Collision Changed the Milky Way Forever
15. The Wolves of Hate Are Loose
16. The Most Ridiculous Halloween Costumes of the Year
17. This Is the Formula for Happiness
18. Water Found on Mars?
19. 6 Astrology Myths to Stop Believing
20. Snake Charmer Chases Monkey After It Snatches His Cobra
21. _____

LIBRARY SECTIONS

1. Advertising
2. African American Studies
3. African Studies
4. Agriculture
5. American Studies
6. Ancient World Studies
7. Anthropology
8. Archaeology
9. Architecture
10. Art
11. Art History
12. Astronomy
13. Automobiles
14. Biography
15. Biology
16. Business and Management
17. Chemistry
18. Children
19. Classics
20. Computer Science
21. Dance
22. Data and Statistics
23. Design
24. Divinity
25. Drama and Theater Studies
26. East Asia Studies
27. Economics
28. Education
29. Engineering and Applied Science
30. Environmentalism
31. Ethics
32. Ethnicity, Race, and Migration
33. Fashion
34. Film
35. Finance
36. Forestry and Environmental Studies
37. Gender and Sexuality Studies
38. Geology and Geophysics
39. Global Affairs
40. Government
41. History, Ancient
42. History, Europe

43. History of Science, Medicine
44. History, United States
45. Inventing and Patents
46. Jobs
47. Judaic Studies
48. Languages
49. Latin American Studies
50. Law
51. Literature
52. Marketing
53. Mathematics
54. Medicine
55. Middle East Studies
56. Music
57. Native American Studies
58. Near Eastern Languages and Civilization

59. News Media—Journalism
60. Nursing
61. Philosophy
62. Photography
63. Physics
64. Poetry
65. Political Science
66. Politics
67. Popular Culture
68. Psychology
69. Public Health
70. Radio
71. Real Estate
72. Religious Studies
73. Renaissance Studies
74. Romance
75. Russian and European Studies
76. Science

77. Self-Help and Inspiration
78. Sexuality
79. Slavic and Baltic Studies
80. Sociology
81. South Asian Studies
82. Southeast Asian Studies
83. Stocks
84. Sustainability
85. Technology
86. Television
87. Theater
88. True Crime
89. Women's Studies
90. Writing and Publishing
91. _____

MAGAZINES

1. *3D Artist*
2. *3D World*
3. *Acoustic Instruments*
4. *All About History*
5. *All About Space*
6. *Airgun Shooter*
7. *Bass Guitar*
8. *Bow International*
9. *Classic Rock*
10. *Clay Shooting*
11. *Comic Heroes*
12. *Computer Arts*
13. *Computer Music*
14. *Crime Scene*
15. *Digital Camera Magazine*

16. *Digital Photographer*
17. *Edge*
18. *Future Music*
19. *GamesMaster*
20. *Guitar Techniques*
21. *History of Royals*
22. *History of War*
23. *Homebuilding and Renovating*
24. *Horrorville*
25. *How It Works*
26. *ImagineFX*
27. *Maximum PC*
28. *Metal Hammer*
29. *Paint and Draw*
30. *PC Gamer*

31. *Period Living*
32. *PhotoShop Creative*
33. *Professional Photography*
34. *Real Crime*
35. *Real Homes*
36. *Retro Gamer*
37. *Rhythm*
38. *Sporting Rifle*
39. *Total Film*
40. *Total Guitar*
41. *Web Designer*
42. *World of Animals*
43. _____

MOVIES THAT HAVE NOT BEEN MADE . . . YET!

1. *The Cat That Ate Dad's Pajamas*
2. *Journey Down the Mississippi in November*
3. *The World's Worst Perfume*
4. *A Well-Read Ghost*
5. *A Chef's Favorite Dish*
6. *Flirting with the Enemy*
7. *Hand in Glove: The Story of a Lady*
8. *Up to Code*
9. *Hairline Fracture*
10. *On Second Thought: A Bachelor's Tale*
11. *Diploma Mill*
12. *The Happiest Tragedy*
13. *Stretching into the Horizon*
14. *The City That Always Sleeps*
15. *While You Were Knocked Out*
16. *Overwhelmed Underwhelmed*
17. *You Can't Stay Here*
18. *Heavy Mist*
19. *Cracked Wide Open*
20. *Birthquake*
21. *The Redemption of the President*
22. *Anarchy at Stillwater*
23. *Anytime, Anywhere, Anything*
24. *The Almost Other Brother*
25. *A Time to Chill*
26. _____

OBJECTS

1. Flashlight
2. Toolbox
3. Catnip toy
4. Magic wand
5. Beaker
6. Globe
7. Empty bottle of wine
8. Ugly mug
9. Cane
10. Box of matches
11. Sculpture
12. Watch
13. Dresser knob
14. Candlestick holder
15. Photo album
16. Handkerchief
17. Marble
18. Diamond ring
19. Passport
20. Baseball
21. Film reel
22. Camera
23. Goggles
24. Wallet
25. Game controller
26. Book
27. Letter opener
28. Paperweight
29. Gun
30. Frying pan
31. Embroidered patch
32. USB thumb drive
33. Ice pick
34. Collar
35. Brush
36. Tea cup
37. Belt
38. Handcuffs
39. Piano wire
40. Diary
41. Quill
42. Doorstop
43. Poker
44. Seed
45. Apron
46. Pill
47. Wind-up toy

48. Headband
49. Cross
50. Lipstick
51. Bandana
52. Cigar box
53. Phone
54. Pipe
55. Pencil
56. Arrow
57. Baton
58. Bracelet
59. Guitar
60. Harmonica
61. Pom-poms
62. Knife

63. Gold ring
64. Porcelain doll
65. Feather
66. Gas can
67. Jewel
68. Measuring tape
69. Brass knuckles
70. Neck pillow
71. Apple
72. Marionette
73. Deck of cards
74. Hat
75. Socks

76. Crystal
77. Wind chime
78. Potted plant
79. Sword
80. Glove
81. Laptop
82. Spoon
83. Trumpet
84. Moving box
85. Buddha statue
86. Scarf
87. Rosary beads
88. Rubik's cube
89. Newspaper

90. Crown
91. Framed photo
92. Scissors
93. Typewriter
94. Treasure chest
95. Bamboo mat
96. Lunchbox
97. Computer chip
98. Trophy
99. Compass
100. Key
101. _____

PREMISES

1. A couple finding a dead body in their own home.

2. Seeing someone jump in front of the train tracks in the subway.

3. Finding a paper bag of money in the mailbox

4. At a restaurant witnessing the chef violently abusing the staff.

5. On vacation at a tropical island watching the sunset—a creepy stranger approaches, bleeding profusely.

6. Helping friends search for their lost dog—discovering it's been stolen by their neighbor.

7. Discovering the ability to hear people's thoughts.

8. Having a chance encounter at a bar with a celebrity who is very different than they appeared.

9. Armed and at the bank while an unexpected robbery is going on.

10. Throwing a large party in honor of a friend who has just been kidnapped.

11. A social worker arriving at a couple's home to take away their children.

12. Getting arrested on the street—charged with murder.

13. Getting arrested at work for embezzlement—definitely did it.

14. Standing by with coworkers while the boss is arrested—he's not guilty, but one of the employees is.

15. While traveling for work, a CEO's identity is stolen.

16. Awakening in a hospital with no memory and no recollection of the person claiming to be the spouse.

17. Discovering the ability to control others' minds.

18. Peering into a neighbor's house and spying a small body tied up.

19. Finding a baby on the doorstep—there's a note with symbols on it.

20. At a rock concert, the band is taken hostage.

21. While developing photographs, discovering photos of a crime.

22. Finding a tracking device in the car and mobile phone.

23. Discovering a new, evolving life form.

24. Winning the lottery as the market crashes and being bullied to return the funds.

25. A teacher informing a couple that their child is a prodigy and claiming they aren't equipped to parent her.

26. Discovering a pinhole camera—in the bedroom.

27. A fortune-teller blackmailing a customer.

28. Purchasing a home that is clearly haunted and dangerous.

29. A down-on-their-luck musician being sure they have found an unpublished/unproduced song from their music icon.

30. Upon waking, a talking spider appears on the pillow and promises three wishes.

31. Receiving a call that a relative has passed away and left billions in an account accessible only after a series of bizarre challenges are solved.

32. In a move, a family dog being accidentally left at a rest stop and finding its way to the family over thousands of miles.

33. Finding out the person from a one-night stand six months ago is pregnant.

34. Discovering the ability to self-heal.

35. While stranded on a deserted island for months, finally seeing a boat in the distance.

36. An ex returning and beginning systematically destroying the new life being built.

37. Checking the safe deposit box and finding nothing but a note: "Gotcha!"

38. A tornado coming through and sweeping everything away—home, neighbors' homes.

39. Discovering that the pets can all talk.

40. Being surprised with a huge surprise birthday party and feeling heart pain.

41. Being proposed to and having to admit to already being married.

42. Waking up to realize today is the exact same one as yesterday—the worst day ever.

43. Discovering your house has been robbed—by a friend.

44. Finding out what heaven is like—not so perfect.

45. Getting the results from a paternity test—you're not related.

46. Being saved from a deadly fall by a stranger.

47. Being asked to not leave the dressing room of a luxury store; on trying the door, finding it's locked from the outside.

48. Discovering certificates proving being given up for adoption at birth.

49. Finding a secret room in your new house full of journals and artifacts from the last several centuries.

50. Learning that your best friend has committed a shocking crime.

51. _____
_____
_____

PRESS CONFERENCE QUESTIONS

1. How long have you been in your field?
2. What drew you to this line of work?
3. Was this what you originally started out wanting to do?
4. Have you made any particular discoveries that you are proud of or, alternatively, wish you hadn't discovered?
5. What inspires you?
6. Can you talk about some of the latest developments in your field?
7. How do these developments affect your day-to-day work?
8. Are there any changes you would like to see taking place?
9. Is there anyone who helped you along the way? A mentor?
10. Could you share one secret to your success?
11. When did you know you wanted this job?
12. What career mistake has given you the biggest lesson?
13. Have you ever felt you've been given a sign that you were on the right path?
14. If you were going to write a book on your field of expertise, what would it be about and be titled?
15. Do you stand behind your work?
16. Do you take time for yourself? If so, how?
17. In your life, who has given you the most support? Do you think you have been good to them in return?
18. What makes you the happiest?
19. Do you feel connected to something larger?
20. Are there mundane things you do to escape?
21. Are you holding secrets for anyone else?
22. Are you more comfortable in solitude or at a party?
23. If you had to give a speech about what you have learned in life, what are some aspects you would include?
24. What is the biggest risk you could take in today's climate?
25. What impresses you the most about your friends?
26. Have you ever wanted to run away?
27. Who is the one person in your life now that you know has your back?
28. What is the best idea you ever had?
29. What are you most excited about?
30. What do you like to read on your own time?
31. What are some examples of your best work?
32. When did you know this is who you wanted to become?
33. _____

PROTAGONISTS

1. Poor physicist
2. Very particular and organized orphan
3. Talkative janitor
4. Forward-thinking psychotherapist
5. Thoughtful plumber
6. Poor single parent
7. Small-minded full-time parent

8. Critical neuroscientist
9. Naive writer
10. Troubled scientist
11. Quirky transgender life-coach
12. Bossy brain surgeon
13. Mean public defender
14. Generous rancher
15. Unusual pastry chef
16. Oddball veterinarian
17. Kind healer
18. Sensitive interior designer
19. Tactful football coach
20. Organized baker
21. Disheveled translator at the UN
22. Assertive small-business owner
23. Accepting psychotherapist
24. Adventurous college counselor
25. Ambitious astrophysicist
26. Quiet economics guru
27. Truthful blogger
28. Conscientious biopic filmmaker
29. Gentle child services social worker
30. Thorough drama coach
31. Reassuring hospital volunteer
32. Considerate world traveler
33. Cooperative antique store
34. Creative librarian
35. Decisive yoga teacher
36. Dependable physics professor
37. Devoted documentary filmmaker
38. Earnest White House correspondent
39. Lazy Fair Trade Certifications Board member
40. Productive passport officer
41. Punctual peace advocate
42. Responsible gun shop owner
43. Imaginative cameraperson
44. Simple travel blogger
45. Independent child
46. Persistent talk show host
47. Bothersome neighbor
48. Helpful museum docent
49. Enterprising art historian
50. Focused cheerleader
51. Congenial president of the United States
52. Recalcitrant football player
53. Depressed grave-digger
54. Exhausted CEO of a Fortune 500 company
55. Distracted chiropractor
56. Poetic trash collector
57. Proud homeless man or woman
58. Genuine Olympic athlete
59. Surly farmer
60. Irritable family counselor
61. Fastidious Department of Transportation personnel
62. Gaudy pawnbroker
63. Adventurous marine biologist
64. Jubilant pharmacist
65. World-renowned art dealer
66. Cheeky used car dealer
67. Classy photographer
68. Sassy judge
69. Illiterate law clerk
70. Patient cashier
71. Thoughtful gardener
72. Generous cleaning person
73. Illiterate chef
74. Acerbic bartender
75. Reserved peace activist
76. Tipsy tailor
77. Careful priest or priestess
78. Curious prison guard

79. Mean chess champion

80. Self-important computer analyst

81. Precise jeweler

82. Innovative illustrator

83. Easygoing environmental activist

84. Able soldier

85. Arrogant banker

86. Sociable accountant

87. Trendy fashion designer

88. Powerful mayor

89. Merry toy manufacturer

90. Quiet animation artist

91. Secretive radio jockey

92. Smart website designer

93. Shy entomologist

94. Triumphant historian

95. Entertaining cruise director

96. Pragmatic sailor

97. Spoiled equestrian

98. No-nonsense massage therapist

99. Aging mechanic

100. Retired oncologist

101. _____

PRODUCTS (MADE-UP)

1. Uncle Rebo's Nectar

2. Trinkles

3. Blur-Water

4. Ball of Floof

5. Square Robot

6. Cereal of Nymphs

7. Sackle-Pumps

8. Aerosol of Aeros

9. Cat-Pleats

10. Change-Scissors

11. Dental-Zips

12. Energy Towers

13. Fairy Toppers

14. Gallon of Instant Jungle

15. Ear Gloss

16. Lip Poppers

17. Mixed Masher

18. Baby Biters

19. Can of No-Shine

20. Oil of Periwinkle

21. Quick Wash Furble

22. Candy Lumps

23. Open-Toed Paddle Hoppers

24. Quick-Peel Banana

25. Zany's Ice Chomps

26. Crawling Crisps

27. Plate Spinners Planner

28. Filing Fingers

29. Eazy Eyes

30. Elfin Pods

31. _____

PUBLIC DOMAIN STORIES

1. *Tales of Space and Time* by H. G. Wells

2. *Japanese Fairy Tales* by Yei Theodora Ozaki

3. *The Mysterious Island* by Jules Verne

4. *Little Women* by Louisa May Alcott

5. *The Mysterious Affair at Styles* by Agatha Christie

6. *Sense and Sensibility* by Jane Austen

7. *Wuthering Heights* by Emily Brontë

8. *Dracula* by Bram Stoker

9. *Romeo and Juliet* by William Shakespeare

10. *The Art of War* by Sun Tzu

11. _____

RELATIONSHIPS

1. Siblings
2. Married
3. Couple
4. Grandparent/grandchild
5. Boss and employee
6. Patient and nurse
7. Doctor and nurse
8. Doctor and patient
9. Lawyer and client
10. Guru and disciple
11. Priest and parishioner
12. Owner of café and waiter
13. Bus/car driver and passenger
14. Pilot and copilot
15. Politician and voter
16. President and cabinet member
17. Astronaut and alien
18. Alien and earthling
19. God and devil
20. God and human
21. Rat and lab assistant
22. Computer and coder
23. Puppet and puppeteer
24. Actor and director
25. Actor and stunt double
26. Popstar and fan
27. Terrorist and hostage
28. Professor and assistant
29. Philosopher and student
30. Judge and lawyer
31. Criminal and victim
32. Newly engaged couple
33. Step-parent and step-child
34. Mother/father-in-law and daughter/son-in-law
35. Coach and athlete
36. Referee and player
37. Governor and taxpayer
38. Newlyweds
39. Newly divorced
40. Vet and pet
41. _____

SETTINGS

1. Stairwell of the Eiffel Tower
2. At the edge of quicksand
3. Barn
4. Train station
5. Wheat field
6. Farmhouse
7. New York City condominium
8. Control room at NASA
9. Poolside
10. Bridge over a Venice canal
11. Houseboat
12. Television studio
13. Armory
14. Army barracks
15. Children's hospital
16. Clinic
17. Massage parlor
18. Burlesque nightclub
19. Kitchen
20. Executive jet
21. Watering hole
22. Abandoned well
23. Gas station
24. Post office
25. Produce section at the grocery store
26. Locker room

27. Trailer park
28. Forest
29. Polluted beach
30. Nature preserve
31. Zoo
32. Dog park
33. Ice cream stand
34. Interrogation room
35. Diner
36. Café
37. Botanical gardens
38. Church courtyard
39. Library
40. Treehouse
41. Mine
42. Ghost town
43. Allegedly haunted hotel
44. Phonebooth
45. Deserted island
46. Tropical jungle
47. Hut on the beach
48. Fork in the road
49. French bakery
50. Royal palace
51. _____

SETTINGS (MADE-UP)

1. Arches of Erowhon
2. Beaches of Trinity Falls
3. The Caverns at Little Bear
4. Delta of the Upside-Down
5. Energy Fields of Clavador
6. Faraway Nix-Town
7. Gorge of Failure
8. High Mountains of Fortitude
9. Interior of the Unknown Plateau
10. Jerryville
11. King Solis's Palace of Challenge
12. The Lakes of Infinite Sadness
13. Moon Colony
14. Nearly There Bordertown
15. The Opal of Opportunity
16. The Pantheon of Grace
17. Quicksand Dunes
18. Rapids of Cherry Hill
19. Searing Lava Run of Sennett's Place
20. Toadtown
21. Underwater Pools of Persecution
22. Vortex of Hades
23. Wallowing Ponds
24. X-Ray Isla
25. Yesterday's River
26. Zenith's Entrance to Evermore
27. Barren Fields of Troubadours
28. The Channels of Light
29. Bright Skull Mountain
30. Quertols Prison
31. _____

STORIES THAT HAVE NEVER BEEN TOLD BEFORE

1. *The Man Who Waited It Out in the Jungle Long Enough to Win a Guinness World Record*

2. *Two Ninjas: One World*

3. *Tears of an Alabama Rooster*

4. *Happiness Can Be Found Everywhere, Even in Your World*

5. *How I Found the End of the World and the Path I Took Back*

6. *What's Up, Mrs. Farmer? Is it Too Late to Visit?*

7. *My Transitioning Transistor is Coming in Loud and Clear*

8. *Everyone Wants to Wear Crocs, They Just Don't Know It*

9. *This Was Only the Second Time He Left, But I Knew It Was for Good*

10. *The Woman of the Wilding: Who We All Want to Be*

11. *Rear Windows and Bad Drivers Make a Bad Combination*

12. *Insinuation Station of the Nation*

13. *Watch Out! They're Coming for You and You Don't Even Know What They Look Like*

14. *Feelings are Overrated—Even for Us Snakes*

15. *How a Porcupine Learned to Live with Herself—True Story*

16. *Everything Is Put in Perspective When The Prospector Comes to Town*

17. *Challenge: A Story You've Never Heard or Seen*

18. *Something Smaller Than a Breadbox. . . .*

19. *Cheers: The Story of a Life That Was Never Supposed to Be Lived*

20. *What They Don't Tell You in Shock Therapy: An Electric Recounting*

21. _____
    _____
    _____

SUGGESTIONS

1. If you could have dinner with one person from history, who would it be and where?

2. What was an embarrassing gift you've been given?

3. What was your favorite childhood meal?

4. What would a perfect first date be like?

5. What did you get a gold star for in school?

6. If you could live in another country, what would your daily life be like there?

7. You wake up inside a television show you've been bingeing; what is it?

8. Did you ever steal anything you felt belonged to you anyway?

9. What's the name of your imaginary best friend from childhood?

10. What will your first day of retirement look like?

11. Is there an object in your life that makes you smile every time you see it?

12. Who would you spill all your secrets to?

13. Give us three things that exemplify your childhood best friend.

14. What is one thing you pack every trip you take?

15. Sum up your morning in one word.

16. You start a punk rock band—what are you called?

17. After getting hit by lightning, you now have what power?

18. What is a word that you hate the sound of? Like "squishy," or "moist," or . . .

19. What makes you feel strong?

20. What is your most prized possession?

21. _____
   _____
   _____

SUPPORTING PLAYERS

1. Petulant child
2. Belligerent teen
3. Rebellious priest
4. Competitive employee
5. Supportive wingman/ wingwoman
6. Teary-eyed clairvoyant
7. Objective economics professor
8. Queasy nurse
9. Gregarious coworker
10. Judicious parent
11. Insightful friend
12. Loyal lover
13. Meticulous caretaker
14. Mature babysitter
15. Juvenile boss
16. Childish sibling
17. Immature aunt
18. Outgoing shop owner
19. Patient counselor
20. Unprofessional police officer
21. Poised prince or princess
22. Lackadaisical instructor
23. Rude computer hacker
24. Polite peer
25. Tell-it-like-it-is assistant

26. Touchy boss
27. Restless nail technician
28. Excitable code-breaker
29. Sloth-like fitness trainer
30. Pessimistic detective
31. Brilliant artist
32. Vibrant artist
33. Award-winning acrobat
34. Even-tempered witch/warlock
35. Intelligent mail clerk
36. Lively receptionist
37. Determined addict
38. Effective speech therapist
39. Funny friend

40. Zoned-out drug dealer
41. Ambling heir
42. Weary author
43. Wistful ballerina
44. Witty carpenter
45. Welcoming talk show host
46. Boastful handwriting expert
47. Messy roommate
48. Masterful pianist
49. Fortunate fairy
50. Passive reporter
51. _____

THEMES

1. Forgiveness
2. Determination
3. Generosity
4. Acceptance
5. Power corrupts
6. Patience
7. Knowledge is power
8. Progress
9. Life is hollow
10. Justice
11. Peace and war
12. Innocence
13. Self-sacrifice
14. Power is evil
15. Persistence
16. Mercy
17. Love conquers all
18. Bravery
19. Discipline
20. Life is a mystery
21. Friendship
22. Tolerance

23. Grace
24. Death is absolute
25. Courage
26. Trustworthiness
27. Compassion
28. Hope springs eternal
29. The search for happiness
30. Perseverance
31. Underdogs can win
32. Gratitude
33. Let go
34. Find your tribe
35. Seek the truth
36. Honor
37. Conquer the mind
38. Integrity
39. We are all one
40. Growing up
41. _____

Notes

Page 31. "One day in the year 1666": Francois Marie Arouet Voltaire, *Éléments,* as translated in *The Book of Days: A Miscellany of Popular Antiquities in Connection with the Calendar,* ed. Robert Chambers, vol. 2 (1888; repr. Charleston, SC: Nabu Press, 2011), 757.

Page 31. "Meditation is a practice": Suze Yalof Schwartz, *Unplug: A Simple Guide to Meditation for Busy Skeptics and Modern Soul Seekers* (New York: Harmony Books, 2017), 23–24.

Page 32. "Steven Spielberg claims that his very best ideas": Julia Cameron, P*The Artist's Way* (New York: Putnam/Tarcher, 1992, 2002), 23.

Page 35. "I'm a meditator": David Lynch, *Catching the Big Fish: Meditation, Consciousness, and Creativity* (New York: Penguin Random House, 2006), 29.

Page 53. "There is a vitality, a life force, an energy": As quoted in Agnes de Mille, *The Life and Work of Martha Graham* (New York: Random House, 1991), 264.

Page 56. "When we speak evil": Publius Syrus, *The Moral Sayings of Publius Syrus, a Roman Slave: From the Latin.* Full text available at https://archive.org/stream/moralsayingspub00lymagoog/moralsayingspub00lymagoog_djvu.txt.

Page 56. "It doesn't matter if your great dare is politics or the PTO": Brené Brown, *Daring Greatly* (New York: Avery, 2012), 167.

Page 77. "I pay no attention": Kate Riggs, *Mozart* (Mankato: Creative Education, 2009), 4.

Page 143. "A premise is rarely a closed statement": Robert McKee, *Story* (New York: Harper Collins, 1997), 212.

Page 143. "'What would happen if . . .' is only one kind of premise": McKee, *Story*, 212.

Page 159. "Beats, changing patterns of human behavior": McKee, *Story*, 217.

Page 174. "Style (and originality perhaps) is really simple honesty": Saks, *Funny Business: The Craft of Comedy Writing* (Cincinnati, OH: Writer's Digest, 1985).

About the Author

© Peter Konerko

JORJEANA MARIE is an author, actress, and teacher. Whether it's writing at Disney (*Mickey and the Roadster Racers*), as a voice actress enacting all the roles in the "New Nancy Drew Diaries" (where Nancy now uses GPS to find her criminals and spends her spare time Googling herself!), or as a produced playwright in NYC, she seeks out strong and interesting protagonists. Her article "Laugh Track," on ways of finding the funny, is featured in the recent *Writer's Digest* "The Comedy Issue" and "Writer's Workbook."

As an actress, she has narrated over two hundred audiobooks (Audie Award-Winner as well as over a dozen Earphones) and can be heard in numerous video games and animated shows. As a teacher, she has taught improv to Emmy- and Oscar-winning actors and beginners alike. She splits her time between New York and Los Angeles.

Index

A

action, incorporating, 133
Ad Agency game, 27–28
Affleck, Ben, 5
Ages list, 186
The Alphabet Game, 154–56
" . . . and" rule
    Ad Agency game, 27–28
    importance of, 24–26
    Pitch It game, 28–29
Angelou, Maya, 22–23
Animal Essence exercise, 136–37
Animals list, 186
Antagonists list, 187
Ask for It exercise, 98–99
Aunt Bertha game, 115
Austin, Gary, 3, 132, 167

B

Blanchett, Cate, 6
Bradbury, Ray, 159
Brown, Brené, 56
Bucket List game, 127–28

C

Cameron, Julia, 32, 89
characters
    Ages list, 186
    Animal Essence exercise, 136–37
    Antagonists list, 187

Aunt Bertha game, 115
Bucket List game, 127–28
change and, 116, 162
Character Shoes game, 60
Character Visit game, 51
Committed to Character game, 58–59
Dear Diary game, 141–42
Emotional Roller Coaster game,
    122–23
Emotional Scrambler game, 124
Endowments list, 189
Flawed game, 117–18
Flaws list, 189–92
Gibberish game, 125–26
Goals game, 126–27
Hidden Agenda game, 132–33
importance of, 4–7, 112–13
Letter to Mother game, 116
Movement in Character warm-up, 59
New Choice game, 130–31
New Year's Resolution game, 128–29
Opposites exercise, 120–21
Protagonists list, 198–200
Rashomon (Point of View) game,
    138–41
Social Media Mania game, 113–15
Supporting Players list, 204–5
Walkabout warm-up, 134–35
World's Worst game, 119–20
Chekhov, Anton, 66

Choose Your Own Intention game, 74–75
Classic Object Work warm-up, 40
Close, Del, 3, 76
Cohan, George M., 159
commitment
    Character Shoes game, 60
    Committed to Character game, 58–59
    criticism and, 8, 76
    importance of, 7–8, 52–57
    Movement in Character warm-up, 59
confidence, 8
conflict, 167
Countdown or 5, 2, 1, :30, :15 game, 179
courage, 56–57
creativity, 8–10
criticism. See judgment

D

Damon, Matt, 5
Davis, Sammy, Jr., 52
Dear Diary game, 141–42
De Niro, Robert, 3
dialogue
    about, 148
    The Alphabet Game, 154–56
    "I Just Have to Say" game, 152–53
    One-Word Story game, 156–58
    Three Lines game, 149–50
    Three Lines—Unstoppable game,
        150–52
Diary Entry—Glad Game Subject, 81

E

editing
    about, 178
    Countdown or 5, 2, 1, :30, :15 game, 179
    time for, 76
Emerson, Ralph Waldo, 82
Emotional Roller Coaster game, 122–23
Emotional Scrambler game, 124
Emotions list, 187–88
Endowments list, 189
enthusiasm
    etymology of, 83–84
    importance of, 82–84
    Mining Magazines game, 90–92
    Passion Player game, 88–89
    Springs on the Soles of Your Feets!
        game, 84–88

Every Breath You Take warm-up, 33
exercises. See games and exercises
expectations. See No Expectations rule
expert, being an
    about, 61–63
    Press Conference game, 64–65

F

Family Portraits game, 100
Fey, Tina, 43
Five Objects—All Very Specific game,
    70–71
Five Objects and One Random Item
    game, 68
Five Objects game, 67
Flawed game, 117–18
Flaws list, 189–92
Freeform Writing as an Object game,
    46–47
fun, 12, 75

G

games and exercises (general)
    approaches to, 13
    creating, 10–11
    as fun, 12
    online information about, 11–12
    with other writers, 29
    repeating, 13
    research, 11–12
    resisting, 14
    timer for, 13, 15, 118
    trust and, 11
games and exercises (specific)
    The Alphabet Game, 154–56
    Animal Essence, 136–37
    Ask for It, 98–99
    Aunt Bertha, 115
    Bucket List, 127–28
    Character Shoes, 60
    Character Visit, 51
    Choose Your Own Intention, 74–75
    Committed to Character, 58–59
    Countdown or 5, 2, 1, :30, :15, 179
    Dear Diary, 141–42
    Diary Entry—Glad Game Subject, 81
    Emotional Roller Coaster, 122–23
    Emotional Scrambler, 124
    Family Portraits, 100

Five Objects, 67
Five Objects—All Very Specific, 70–71
Five Objects and One Random
   Item, 68
Flawed, 117–18
Freeform Writing as an Object, 46–47
Genre Swap, 170–71
Gibberish, 125–26
The Glad Game, 79–80
Goals, 126–27
Good/Bad/Worst/Fixed, 167–68
Headlines, 144–45
Hidden Agenda, 132–33
"I Just Have to Say," 152–53
It's Not Just . . ., 69
Letter to Mother, 116
Making a Monologue, 41–42
Meditation, 35–36
Message in a Monologue, 176
Mining Magazines, 90–92
Motel, 163–65
Movie-Making Machine, 171–72
New Choice, 130–31
New Year's Resolution, 128–29
One-Word Story, 156–58
Opposites, 120–21
Paint the Scenery, 110–11
Passion Player, 88–89
Pick an Object, Any Object!, 39
Pitch It, 28–29
Premises—Built to Order, 146–47
Press Conference, 64–65
Raise the Stakes, 160–62
Rashomon (Point of View), 138–41
See It, Be It!, 34–35
Set It Up!, 50
Soap Opera, 173
Social Media Mania, 113–15
Springs on the Soles of Your Feets!,
   84–88
Three Lines, 149–50
Three Lines—Unstoppable, 150–52
Twist of Theme, 177
Twists, 165–66
World's Worst, 119–20
Yes, Let's, 22–23
Your Local Bookstore, 103–7
Your Local Library, 101–2

genres
   about, 169–70
   Genre Swap game, 170–71
   list, 192
   Movie-Making Machine game, 171–72
   Soap Opera game, 173
Gibbard, Ben, 156
Gibberish game, 125–26
gifting, 25, 55
The Glad Game, 79–80
Goals game, 126–27
Good/Bad/Worst/Fixed game, 167–68
Graham, Martha, 53–54

H
Hawking, Stephen, 148
Headlines game, 144–45
Headlines list, 193
Hemingway, Ernest, 30
Hidden Agenda game, 132–33
Hitchcock, Alfred, 96
Hoffman, Philip Seymour, 6

I
ideas
   Ask for It exercise, 98–99
   definition of, 97
   Family Portraits game, 100
   flow and, 38, 108
   generating, 97–98
   importance of, 96–97
   letting go of, 108
   Your Local Bookstore game, 103–7
   Your Local Library game, 101–2
   See also inspiration
"I Just Have to Say" game, 152–53
improv
   benefits of, 180–81
   definition of, 3
   flexibility of, 11
   focusing on partner in, 49
   history of, 3
   jokes in, 71
   requirements for, 15
   rules in, 4
   scenes in, 93, 149
   vulnerability and, 2
   See also games and exercises;
      warm-ups

impulses, trusting, 11
inspiration
    date with, 89
    personalizing, 105
    See also ideas
intention
    Choose Your Own Intention game,
        74–75
    of having fun, 75
    Readying Ritual warm-up, 73–74
    setting, 72–73
It's Not Just . . . game, 69

J

Johnstone, Keith, 3, 18
judgment
    appreciation vs., 80
    commitment and, 8, 76
    Diary Entry—Glad Game Subject, 81
    giving up, 44, 76–79
    The Glad Game, 79–80

K

Kurosawa, Akira, 138

L

Lange, Dorothea, 174
Letter to Mother game, 116
Library Sections list, 193–94
listening
    benefits of, 48–49
    Character Visit game, 51
    as observation, 48
    Set It Up! game, 50
lists (general)
    benefits of, 185
    creating, 178, 185
    making, 181
lists (specific)
    Ages, 186
    Animals, 186
    Antagonists, 187
    Emotions, 187–88
    Endowments, 189
    Flaws, 189–92
    Genres, 192
    Headlines, 193
    Library Sections, 193–94
    Magazines, 194–95

Movies That Have Not Been Made . . .
        Yet!, 195
    Objects, 195–96
    Premises, 196–97
    Press Conference Questions, 198
    Products (Made-Up), 200
    Protagonists, 198–200
    Public Domain Stories, 200
    Relationships, 201
    Settings, 201–2
    Settings (Made-Up), 202
    Stories That Have Never Been Told
        Before, 203
    Suggestions, 204
    Supporting Players, 204–5
    Themes, 205
Lynch, David, 35, 98

M

Magazines list, 194–95
Making a Monologue game, 41–42
McCarthy, Melissa, 3
McKee, Robert, 5, 143–44, 159–60
meditation
    alternatives to, 32, 36
    benefits of, 31
    exercise, 35–36
    starting out, 31
Message in a Monologue game, 176
Mining Magazines game, 90–92
mistakes, 43–45
moment, being in the
    about, 30–32
    Every Breath You Take warm-up, 33
    Meditation exercise, 35–36
    See It, Be It! exercise, 34–35
monologues
    Gibberish game, 125–26
    Making a Monologue game, 41–42
    Message in a Monologue, game, 176
Motel game, 163–65
Movement in Character warm-up, 59
Movie-Making Machine game, 171–72
Movies That Have Not Been Made . . .
        Yet! list, 195
Mozart, Wolfgang, 77

N

New Choice game, 130–31
New Year's Resolution game, 128–29
Nicholson, Jack, 3
Nielson, Leslie, 143
no, saying, 18–20, 21
No Expectations rule
  about, 37–38
  Classic Object Work warm-up, 40
  Freeform Writing as an Object game, 46–47
  Making a Monologue game, 41–42
  Pick an Object, Any Object! game, 39

O

Objects list, 195–96
One-Word Story game, 156–58
Opposites exercise, 120–21

P

Paint the Scenery game, 110–11
partners, writing with, 14, 49, 65, 156–58
Passion Player game, 88–89
peas in a pod-type scenes, 21
Pick an Object, Any Object! game, 39
Pitch It game, 28–29
playfulness, 19
plot and structure
  about, 159–60
  Good/Bad/Worst/Fixed game, 167–68
  Motel game, 163–65
  Raise the Stakes game, 160–62
  Twists game, 165–66
Postal Service, 156
promises
  about, 143–44
  Headlines game, 144–45
  list, 196–97
  Premises—Built to Order exercise, 146–47
Press Conference game, 64–65
Press Conference Questions list, 198
Products (Made-Up) list, 200
Protagonists list, 198–200
Public Domain Stories list, 200

Q

questions, avoiding, 56

R

Radner, Gilda, 37
Raise the Stakes game, 160–62
Rashomon (Point of View) game, 138–41
Readying Ritual warm-up, 73–74
reality, grounding work in, 54, 148
recording devices, 15
Relationships list, 201
relaxation, 47
Renard, Jules, 169
rewriting, 178–79

S

Saks, Sol, 159, 174
Schwartz, Suze Yalof, 31
See It, Be It! exercise, 34–35
Seinfeld, Jerry, 48
Seneca, 72
Set It Up! game, 50
settings
  importance of, 109
  lists, 201–2
  Paint the Scenery game, 110–11
  Set It Up! game, 50
Shakespeare, William, 2, 3, 134
Sills, Paul, 3
Simon, Neil, 178
Soap Opera game, 173
Social Media Mania game, 113–15
specificity
  Five Objects—All Very Specific game, 70–71
  Five Objects and One Random Item game, 68
  Five Objects game, 67
  importance of, 66–67
  It's Not Just . . . game, 69
Spielberg, Steven, 32, 159
Spolin, Viola, 3, 61
Springs on the Soles of Your Feets! game, 84–88
Stories That Have Never Been Told Before list, 203
Strode, Muriel, 109
structure. See plot and structure
Suggestions list, 204
Supporting Players list, 204–5
Syrus, Publius, 56

T

Tamborello, Jimmy, 156
Tartt, Donna, 39
Tharp, Twyla, 76, 77
Theatre Games, 3
themes
    about, 174–75
    list, 205
    Message in a Monologue game, 176
    Twist of Theme game, 177
Theron, Charlize, 6
Three Lines game, 149–50
Three Lines—Unstoppable game, 150–52
timer, 13, 15, 118
tone, 20
trust
    Freeform Writing as an Object game,
        46–47
    importance of, 11, 43–45
turning points, 159–60
Twist of Theme game, 177
Twists game, 165–66

V

Voltaire, 31

W

Walkabout warm-up, 134–35
Walker, Alice, 112
warm-ups (general)
    importance of, 168
    purpose of, 47
    for writing, 168
warm-ups (specific)
    Classic Object Work, 40
    Every Breath You Take, 33
    Movement in Character, 59
    Readying Ritual, 73–74
    Walkabout, 134–35
Wilder, Billy, 159
World's Worst game, 119

Y

yes, saying
    importance of, 18–21
    Yes, Let's game, 22–23
    See also "... and" rule
Your Local Bookstore game, 103–7
Your Local Library game, 101–2